CHANGING LINES

OTHER BOOKS

by Robert Leichtman, M.D. & Carl Japikse

Active Meditation: The Western Tradition

Forces of the Zodiac

The Art of Living (five volumes)

The Life of Spirit (five volumes)

Healing Lines

Ruling Lines

Connecting Lines

by Robert Leichtman, M.D.

From Heaven to Earth (6 books)

by Carl Japikse

The Light Within Us

Exploring the Tarot

The Hour Glass

The Tao of Meow

The Biggest Tax Cheat in America is the I.R.S.

CHANGING LINES

*A New Interpretation
of the I Ching
For Personal
and Spiritual Growth*

by Robert R. Leichtman, M.D.
and Carl Japikse

ARIEL PRESS
Atlanta, Georgia

No royalties are paid on this book

This book is made possible
by an anonymous gift
to the Publications Fund of Light

ISBN 0-89804-093-0

The I Ching

The I Ching is one of the best systems of "practical philosophy" ever devised. Philosophy is meant to be the pursuit of truth and wisdom. The word itself means "the love of knowledge." But modern philosophy has lost track of its roots. Too often, the pursuit of truth has been replaced by a debate of ideas. Debates can be fascinating, of course, but they tend to polarize thinking, not unite it. As a result, modern philosophy has become fragmented and disconnected, leading to such aberrations of thought as existentialism.

Worst of all, the study of philosophy has become so specialized that it no longer speaks to the average person, even the well-educated average person. It has become impractical. The great ideas of philosophy no longer shape daily thinking and behavior as they once did. Philosophy has become abstruse and esoteric, the plaything of theorists living in the proverbial ivory tower.

This is not what philosophy is meant to be. It is meant to be a practical source of values, mental principles, and guidance upon which intelligent people can base their thinking. It should be accessible at least to the educated, if not to every man and woman in the market place. Ideally, it should be a body of ideas that can be easily consulted and relied upon for a determination of basic values, self-examination, and all types of decision making.

It is interesting that the I Ching has been gaining popularity in the West at the same time that our own philosophical systems are becoming more and more arcane. The average intelligent person senses a need for a practical philosophical system, even if the academics and intellectuals do not. And so an increasing number of people are turning to the I Ching, and discovering that it embodies a great deal of truth and insight that can be easily tapped.

The I Ching is a "practical" system because it can be consulted for practical insight and solutions into the ordinary problems of daily living—business decisions, health problems, the challenge of raising children, and so on. Those who do not understand the I Ching sometimes think of it as a system of fortune telling, but it is not. It is a philosophical system that has been developed by some of the greatest minds China has produced. The fact that it can be used by people of average intelligence to help make sense of their lives, as well as the highly educated, only serves to broaden its value, not diminish it.

The Chinese have worked with the I Ching for thousands of years. In the West, we have worked with it for about fifty years, and only intensely for half of that time. It was Carl Jung's work with the I Ching, more than anything else, that brought this remarkable system to the attention of a large number of people.

Because of the relatively short time we have worked with this system, most people still find it somewhat puzzling to use at times. This is because the commentaries on the I Ching have all been translations of the original Chinese texts, written by

Chinese philosophers using the Chinese language and Chinese thought patterns to communicate with Chinese. This is perfectly normal. But a Westerner wanting insight into how to deal with a cranky neighbor may find it a little daunting to try to understand what the I Ching is answering, if using one of the standard texts.

Recognizing this problem, we decided it was time to do something to correct it. In specific, we saw the enormous potential of using the modern computer to help make the ancient guidance of the I Ching even more practical for the Western mind.

The object was not just to program the computer to construct the hexagrams by random process; after all, this is something that can be done just as easily with three coins! The purpose of computerizing the I Ching was to create a series of modules that could be rapidly accessed by the computer, depending upon the kind of question the user wished to ask. In this way, the commentary of each hexagram could be specifically tailored to the kind of inquiry being made.

In other words, if the user wished to ask a question about health, he or she would direct the computer to select the health module. If the question pertained to relationships, the user would select that module on the computer's menu. The question would then be typed in, the hexagram generated by random selection, and the appropriate commentary would appear.

All that remained to be done was develop a computer program—and to write the text for several different modules!

The computer program, *I Ching On Line,* was developed by James D. Davis, Ph.D., a retired professor of mathematics from Fairleigh Dickinson University. His program for the IBM PC and compatibles first appeared in 1989 and was greeted with high critical acclaim. Dr. Davis was in the process of developing a companion program for the Macintosh when he died.

James Watson, a computer expert at NC Assistant, stepped in, developing a program that takes advantage of the Macintosh's unique capabilities.

This book is the text of the fourth and final module developed. It deals exclusively with understanding personal and spiritual growth.

The first module, dealing with health questions, was issued in 1989. The book containing the text of that module is called *Healing Lines.* The second module is designed to support the decision making process, both in business and personal life. The book containing the text is called *Ruling Lines.* The third module, issued in *Connecting Lines,* uses the I Ching to gain insight into right relationships.

In writing the text for each of these books, we have avoided making a direct translation. Instead, we intuitively "dissected" each hexagram and examined it in its original, archetypal form, then restated these basic ideas so that they apply directly to questions about interpersonal relationships, in terms that can be understood by modern Westerners.

Throughout all four modules, our goal is to help make the I Ching the tool of practical philosophy it was designed to be.

We make no apologies for clarity and the specific focus we have given the text. We are fully aware that many specialists in the I Ching feel that its great strength is its vagueness, which forces the user to utilize his or her intuition. But truth and wisdom are never vague or confusing. They are always simple, clear, and insightful. It is usually a sign of intellectual laziness to fail to make the attempt to communicate this simplicity, clarity, and vision to others in easily understood terms.

Ideally, the text that follows is meant to be used as an adjunct to *I Ching On Line.* Nevertheless, we also know that many people do not own a personal computer, or perhaps do not have a model which will run the program. These people can still use the text for growth—and the others in the set—by using the commentary in this book to interpret the hexagrams they generate by more traditional methods.

Our work is done. Now yours begins. The I Ching can become a source of practical philosophy for you only if you use it for that purpose. If you ask the I Ching silly, irreverent questions, it will give you flippant answers. If you try to use it as a crutch or a scapegoat, it will in essence tell you to stop using it until you are more honest in your pursuit of knowledge. But if you use it sincerely, to try to make sense out of the difficult, confusing issues of life, you will discover a source of unlimited guidance and insight.

The I Ching is meant to be used. Use it wisely, and you will see the results in more intelligent decisions!

How The I Ching Works

The I Ching is a system of archetypal forces, based on the principles of duality and the constancy of change. In China, the component forces of this duality are *yin* and *yang*. In English, we might call them positive and negative, male and female, or point and counterpoint.

The philosophers of ancient China observed that duality and change do not occur capriciously. The phenomena of life arise from a dynamic interaction of dualities. For this reason, there cannot be growth without resistance—or opportunity without hardship, success without failure.

To put this principle in terms of change, as one situation improves, another will decline. As one issue evolves, a second will decay. As the life of one movement grows in vitality, a competitive movement will lose momentum. As the level of competence in one group rises, it sinks in another.

The principle of duality governs all movements in life. And as these dual forces interact with one another, they generate complex change.

Since the Chinese language is based on pictographs, rather than letters, it was natural for the philosophers to translate this idea into images. But these are very abstract images, as befits the basic concept of duality. The symbol for active force was a single straight line; the symbol for passive force was a broken line.

THE EIGHT TRIGRAMS

Heaven

Lake

Fire

Thunder

Wind

Water

Mountain

Earth

11

The first combination of these solid and broken lines was to form a set of eight trigrams, each containing three lines. These eight trigrams are illustrated on the previous page. To these trigrams, philosophers began attaching meanings and interpretations, just as the ancient astrologers ascribed meanings to the constellations in the sky. And so, the trigram Heaven took on the meaning of raw creative energy and universal purpose. The trigram Fire, by contrast, took on the meaning of awareness—the fiery mind and brilliance.

Eventually, these trigrams were put together, one on top of the other, to form hexagrams. The upper trigram came to represent the larger picture of any situation—the view from heaven, as it were. The lower trigram came to represent the individualized focus of our daily problems.

There are a total of sixty-four hexagrams, but sixty-four is not the important number. Two is. Each hexagram is the direct result of duality and change, because each hexagram is composed of six lines, each of which is either solid or broken. Positive or negative. Active or passive.

As the system evolved, the ancient Chinese philosophers realized that few situations in life remain stagnant for very long. The hexagrams are not just abstract images—they are symbols for dynamic, active forces. And so every hexagram has the potential to change into any one of the other sixty-three, or remain static.

The first hexagram represents the basic definition of a situation, as it exists now.

The second indicates what the inherent energies of the situation are leading to.

It is this capacity to represent moving, living forces that makes the I Ching ("I Ching" means "Book of Change") such a valuable tool of practical philosophy. Each hexagram is linked with a specific archetypal force affecting human life. As we use the I Ching to understand our problems and challenges, we begin to perceive what dynamic forces are active in our life, and where they are leading us. Patterns emerge, leading to insight.

Using the I Ching is very simple. If you have a computer and *I Ching On Line,* just call up the program, type in your question, and follow the directions to generate the hexagrams. [For more detailed help, refer to the instructions which come with the program.]

If you do not have a computer, you can generate the hexagrams by using three coins. Having thought of your question (it is best to write it down), you construct the hexagrams by tossing the coins six times. Each time you toss the three coins, there are four possible ways they can land:

• All three coins can be heads. This represents a broken line, changing. [▬▬ ▬▬ •]

• All three coins can be tails. This represents a solid line, changing. [▬▬▬▬ •]

• Two coins can be heads and one a tail. This represents an unchanging solid line. [▬▬▬▬]

• Two coins can be tails and one a head. This represents an unchanging broken line. [▬▬ ▬▬]

The Chinese work from the bottom up. Therefore, the first toss generates the bottom line of the hexagram. The second toss generates the line above it, and so on, until all six lines are determined, from bottom to top.

It is helpful to develop some kind of annotation indicating changing lines. This can be a dot (●) to the right of the line or, as we use in the computer program, a triangle (▲). The changing lines enable you to construct the second hexagram, or resolution. All unchanging lines in the first hexagram remain the same in the second hexagram. But a solid line that is changing in the first hexagram becomes a broken line in the second, and a broken line that is changing becomes a solid line. These changing lines indicate the principle of duality in action, moving from pole to pole.

In other words, hexagram #28, Crisis, is composed of a broken, four solid, and a broken line, reading from the bottom up. If lines 2 and 3 are changing, then they create a completely different hexagram, #45, Planning, which is composed of three broken, two solid, and a broken line, from the bottom up.

28 ➤ 45

The first hexagram defines the issue at hand. Each changing line reveals the subtle energies influencing conditions. The second hexagram indicates how the situation will be resolved.

If there are no changing lines in the first hexagram, then the situation is considered static. A second hexagram is not constructed.

In advanced uses of the I Ching, a third hexagram is generated as well. This is called the *nuclear* hexagram. It is derived by taking the second, third, and fourth lines (from the bottom up) of the first hexagram and transliterating them as the first, second, and third lines of the nuclear hexagram. The third, fourth, and fifth lines of the original hexagram are then transliterated as the fourth, fifth, and sixth lines of the nuclear.

There are only sixteen hexagrams which serve as nuclear hexagrams, each one being produced by four different hexagrams. These are obviously the most potent hexagrams of the sixty-four, representing primary archetypal forces. In general, the nuclear hexagram indicates the ideal methodology to use in handling the situation at hand.

Once these three hexagrams are generated, the process of interpretation can begin. If aided by *I Ching On Line,* the appropriate commentary will flash on the screen with just a touch of a key or the click of a mouse. But even without a computer, the process of interpretation is still relatively easy.

Determine the number of each of the three hexagrams. Then, starting with the first hexagram, turn to the appropriate page in this book and read the commentary on the left hand page. This commentary is broken into three sections. The first is a general, overall statement about the forces affecting the subject of your inquiry. The second comments on the nature of the resistance you may be experiencing toward the demands of growth. The third comments on the next step you need to take to cooperate with the work of growth.

Read these comments carefully and reflect on them. It is often wise to reread the text several times, to make sure you fully understand it.

Next, read whatever text on the right hand page corresponds to the changing lines that apply to your consultation. In other words, if lines 2 and 3 are changing, read only the text for lines 2 and 3. Discount the rest. Should there be no changing lines, read only the text entitled "Unchanging."

Once you have digested the commentary for the first hexagram and its changing lines, turn to the pages which comment on the second hexagram, the Resolution. Read the text on the left-hand page, but do not read any of the changing lines.

Finally, consult the text for the nuclear hexagram, again reading just the text on the left-hand page.

If you are serious about understanding more about yourself and life in general, it would be a good idea to keep a record of your I Ching consultations. Write down your question, list the hexagrams that are generated, and then make notes about the insights and conclusions you derive from reading the text. Date each entry, so you can refer back to it easily at a later time.

Of course, if you are using *I Ching On Line,* the computer does all this record keeping for you.

Because of the unique module feature of *I Ching On Line,* it is usually relatively easy to interpret the answers you get while using the text of *Changing Lines.* The text is written on the assumption that the user is asking a question pertaining to personal or spiritual growth. It is not the intent of the I Ching to dictate to the user exactly what he or she should or should not do, however. The purpose of the I Ching is to reveal the larger context in which the situation at hand is unfolding, so that the decision made will be the most intelligent one possible. As long as the question fits these parameters, the answers provided by the text in *Changing Lines* should be relatively straightforward.

This is not to say that this text cannot be used for questions that do not strictly fit this pattern. Like any good system of divination, this text can be used to answer any legitimate question. But the farther afield the question wanders from the focus of the module—understanding personal and spiritual growth—the more intuitive the interpretation will have to be to arrive at the truth.

In this regard, it is important to understand that spiritual growth is primarily an inner phenomenon. It deals far more with values, motives, goals, and attitudes than it does with the triumphs and catastrophes of daily living. There is often a relationship between inner growth and outer events, of course, but the true focus of our growth is always to be found within our character—and our relationship with our higher, spiritual self.

A lot of people are confused about what growth really is. They think that if they get in touch with their feelings, they have done something important. Or if they turn off their conscience and learn to manipulate others without guilt, that they have become a better person. The intellectually inclined believe that they can grow through intensive study or analysis.

This is just nonsense, of course. Real growth requires the introduction of something new and noble into our character and behavior—a new skill, a greater ability to forgive others, a new measure of patience, and so on. Growth occurs slowly, through self-mastery: the acquisition of greater discipline, a stronger ability to make intelligent sacrifices, and a more profound capacity to cooperate with others.

The product of growth is maturity. Growth must deal with our immaturity and childishness, but it never glorifies it. It glorifies wisdom, goodwill, and competence.

Of course, not everyone agrees with this concept of growth, even though it makes good sense. Some people are so confused about growth that they think we must revert to childhood in order to grow. So they advocate immaturity. They teach people to fantasize, escape, blame, and shirk responsibility. If you have been exposed to any of these "experts," it may take you some time to adapt to the ideas in this book.

For this—and other good reasons—be sure to take whatever amount of time is necessary to formulate an intelligent, penetrating question. Do not rush through this preliminary stage. Think carefully. Reflect on your situation. What do you need to know?

Some people do not use questions. They assume that the I Ching knows better than they do what they need to hear, so they simply toss the coins without troubling themselves with a question.

This is not desirable. The I Ching does know what you need to hear, but it is incapable of communicating it to you unless you create a strong invocation for the answer. This invocation is created by focusing a potent need to know. The more intelligently and precisely you formulate your question, the better the results will be.

In using *Changing Lines,* it is also good to keep in mind that the I Ching will try to help you if your question is poorly framed. If you try to ask a question such as, "Why does my husband resent my interest in growing and interfere with my growth?" the I Ching is likely to answer, in so many words, "Your central lesson is learning to love your husband as he is, not resent him or blame him for your inadequacies." In point of fact, it will probably give you a stern lecture about blaming others—and encourage you to see that you and you alone control how much—or how little— you will learn.

The best kind of questions are those that will lead you toward a deeper understanding of your potential for growth:

What spiritual qualities can help me become a better parent?

What spiritual lessons am I learning as I strive to cope with the pressures at work?

What are the issues of growth behind the physical problem I have?

How can I best turn this physical handicap into a source of personal growth?

What does it mean to act with maturity in the situation I am struggling with?

How can I express more of my inner nobility in the face of the criticism I am receiving at work?

What are the roots of my poor self-esteem?

How can I summon the strength I need to cope with the embarrassment that is occurring?

What do I need to learn about the life of the higher self?

Just about any question pertaining to your growth is fine, so long as it does not require a "yes" or "no" answer. The I Ching is not especially suited to yes or no questions; its purpose is to provide insight and understanding.

You can even ask nonpersonal questions. The principles of growth apply to groups as well as individuals, so you can ask questions such as:

What does our company need to learn in order to improve its relations with its customers?

What does the United States need to learn about the role it is meant to play in the world?

What must scientists learn in order to help science overcome its preoccupation with the materialistic dimensions of life?

What is the best way for humanity to confront the problems of intolerance and bigotry that divide it?

It is important, however, to show respect for the I Ching. For this reason, do not ask the same question repeatedly, either because you did not understand the original answer or (the more common motivation) because you did not like the answer. If you are confused by an answer, it is perfectly all right to ask for a clarification—just do not ask the exact same question again.

As an example, assume you have asked: "How can I learn to be more patient in dealing with others?" Hexagram 43, Firm Resolve, informs you: "You are too easily manipulated and controlled by others to develop a firm resolve of your own." If you are unsure how this applies to developing patience, ask a second question: "How does being vulnerable to the manipulations of others hurt my efforts to become more patient?" A different hexagram will probably help you see that your impatience is, in large part, a reaction of irritability to the impatience and hurried pace of others. You need to learn to set your own rhythm and pace for self-expression.

In fact, one question will often lead to a whole series of other questions, just as a tiny pebble thrown into the middle of a pond will produce ripple after ripple of concentric emanations. Keep alert for possible questions and pursue the implications of your query—and its answer—to the furthest extent possible.

The I Ching will never tire of your questions, as long as they are valid and sincere. You are limited only by your own imagination—and your personal need to know.

A Word of Caution

The one thing you can be sure of is that the I Ching will answer your question! This is why it is important to formulate it precisely, write it down, and keep a record of it. The I Ching will not answer the question you *meant* to ask, nor the question you *should have* asked. It will answer the question you actually did ask, as you worded it.

The question you ask becomes frozen in time, once you have generated the hexagrams that answer it. You cannot go back after the fact and reword your question—or reinterpret it because a different question will seem to fit your interpretation of the answer better! It may seem unnecessary to make a point as obvious as this, but sometimes it is the most obvious aspects of life that cause us the most trouble. So it is with the I Ching. The most common cause of confusion in using this system is poor memory. People have an enormous capacity for self-deception, and this extends to asking questions of the I Ching. Once they begin reading the commentary, they often unconsciously change the question they asked—even if they have a written record of it! They alter the question in small ways so that the answer is more favorable to them—or at least less threatening.

As an example, let's say you ask the question: "What will be the outcome of my dispute with my neighbor?" The answer might indicate that the dispute itself is a silly overreaction to an imagined insult. The result will therefore be a continued estrangement between the two of you, until you decide your reaction was indeed silly and make amends. Given your present attitude, you might then conclude that there is nothing to do, since it is clear your neighbor is not going to give in. But the question was not, "When will my neighbor admit he was wrong?" It was: "What will be the outcome of my dispute with my neighbor?" And the answer, quite correctly, indicated that the current schism will continue until you have a change of heart. To understand the answer, therefore, you need to stick to the original question—not make up a new one that fits your need for self-deception!

Obviously, it is of great importance to eliminate this kind of self-deception in using the I Ching. Make a written record of your question, and then refer back to it again and again as you read the commentary and formulate your interpretation of it. If you do not understand the question, after all, it will be impossible to understand the answer!

In using the I Ching, the keynote should always be self-examination. We are looking for new insight into the inner workings of the events and problems of our life—not for new excuses, or new scapegoats, or new rationalizations. If you are prone to self-deception, the first question you need to ask the I Ching is: "How can I best protect myself from my self-deception?" Only when this question is fully answered, and acted upon, should you then proceed with others.

Divine Intelligence

In using the I Ching, the big question to the Westerner is always: "How does this thing work?" We have elevated skepticism to such a high level that almost everyone asks this question when first exposed to the I Ching. Curiously, it is not a common question in China. As a culture, the Chinese are not puzzled by how the I Ching works. The only thing that puzzles them is why the average Westerner makes such a big fuss about it!

They have a point. The Judeo-Christian tradition is the major moral and philosophical basis for thinking in the West; it is common for Westerners to profess a belief in the omnipresence, omnipotence, and omniscience of God. "Omniscience" means not only that God is all-knowing, but on a more practical level, that divine intelligence pervades everything. Whether we are at worship, in our car, at home, or at the grocery, we are surrounded and interpenetrated by divine intelligence (and love and power!) at all times.

Isn't it odd, therefore, that there are so many people who will stand up in church or temple and proclaim divine omniscience, then act as though they left it all behind the moment they stepped outside! But they do—they believe in luck, in random sequences, and in accidents, not in divine omniscience. Frankly, it's not a record that any of us should be proud of.

Divine intelligence is designed to give us the answers we seek. If we are sufficiently enlightened we should be able to discern these answers from any common phenomenon of life—as Brother Lawrence did centuries ago as he watched the leaves fall from trees in autumn and came to understand God's benevolent love and protection.

Since most of us are not this enlightened, special systems have been developed over the eons to help us communicate more easily with divine intelligence. The I Ching is one of these systems. It works because divine intelligence pervades all of life and every event of life, even something as trivial as the "random" throw of three coins or the way in which you strike your computer keyboard six times in succession.

The random action of throwing the coins or striking computer keys is not what triggers the right response; it merely helps us get our own wish life and preconceived ideas out of the way, so that we do not control the process. Once we are unable to consciously influence the selection process of the hexagrams, then divine intelligence is able to take over. Time after time, the right hexagrams are generated to answer our questions.

It is for this reason that we need to take the answers the I Ching provides seriously. And we must also always keep in mind the full context of our questions and answers.

In a very real sense, our personal world is a small but complete universe which exists as a part of the larger universe of our family, our work, our community, our nation, and humanity as a whole. As we develop personal problems, we can only understand them if we are able to see them in the larger context of these bigger spheres of influence. This is true whether the problem involves health, business, relationships, or just our own ethics and inner stability.

The I Ching is designed to help us see our connections to these larger spheres. We may believe that our problem exists only within the microcosm of our private world, but in truth the solution, whatever it is, always lies in the macrocosm. Unless we can reach out to the macrocosm and discover what the solution is, it will evade us.

Divine intelligence is not just a huge cosmic brain. It is a force field of intelligence, filled with living, dynamic energies. These energies are what are known as "archetypal forces." They are the abstract forces from which everything that is has emerged.

Love, wisdom, and power are the three most basic of these forces. Others include grace, joy, beauty, peace, harmony, and abundance. Whenever we have a problem, it is a sign that we lack one of these archetypal forces, or are misusing it. We will not be able to find it within our own private world, however. We must reach out to the macrocosm for it.

The I Ching is one of the great tools for guiding us to the right force and helping us connect with it. In fact, the inner structure of the I Ching makes it clear that this system was designed with just this purpose in mind. The lower trigram in each hexagram represents the microcosm—our private world and needs. The higher trigram represents the inner dimensions of life, the view from heaven. It does not reveal our personal world, but the larger macrocosm in which we live and move and have our being.

Given this basic structure, there are many subtle clues that can help us comprehend the I Ching more completely. It is often useful, for example, to examine each trigram in a hexagram and go back to its original meanings. Hexagram #28, for example, is composed of the trigram for joy in the upper position and the trigram for gentle influences in the lower one. By seeing the component parts in this way, it is easier to understand why this particular hexagram is called "Crisis." The tremendous power above may overwhelm the modest capacity for self-expression below, but if we are able to stretch our skills and talents beyond their normal ability, we can likewise seize an unparalleled opportunity. It is the archetypal energies themselves that create the danger, as they intersect—but it is up to us to determine if these forces will produce a breakthrough, or a breakdown.

This illustrates a point that needs emphasis. Being symbols of archetypal forces, no hexagram is either good or bad. They are all divine. It is up to us to determine how they will be used. If we use these forces wisely, they will be productive. If we use them selfishly, they will be restrictive. The choice is up to us. Our future lies not in the hexagrams themselves, but in our capacity to harness their potential intelligently.

Some of the titles we have chosen for the hexagrams may at times sound ominous: Inner Conflict, Loss, Sabotage, and Hypocrisy. Others may appeal to us much more: Idealism, Enlightenment, and Gain. But these are just labels for forces which are neither positive nor negative. They are building blocks to be used creatively. A wise person will recognize as much potential for advancement in a time of Loss as in a time of Gain, and will act accordingly.

Another key to interpreting the hexagrams is what is known as "ruling lines." A ruling line is something like the accented syllable or syllables in a word: it is the line (or sometimes two lines) that dominates all the other lines in the hexagram. In most texts, the ruling lines are indicated as part of the commentary. We have not done so in the text for *Changing Lines* or any other module, and for a very simple reason. In many consultations of the I Ching, the ruling line will not even appear. Yet if there are three changing lines, one will be dominant for that question, even if none of the changing lines happens to be the natural ruler. If a ruling line has already been picked, it does not encourage the user to try to determine the dominant line. So we have left out the ruling lines, in the hope that the more ambitious users of this text will develop the intuitive habit of determining the true ruler, question by question.

As you read the changing lines, therefore, try to weigh which one is the strongest influence on your situation. It may be perfectly obvious, or it may be obscure. But often once you determine which line is the true ruling force, it gives you the clue you need to interpret the rest of the message. It lets you embrace the inner forces that are at work in this situation.

Ultimately, this is what the I Ching is meant to be:

a barometer of the inner forces which influence us individually and collectively. Treat it with respect, but do not be in awe of it. It is a tool that intelligent people use to understand life. If at any point in your use of the I Ching you are unsure of how to proceed next, do not become flustered. Always remember that you have at your disposal one of the greatest tools of divination ever invented. Just ask the I Ching to show you what to do next—and it will!

A NUMBERED GUIDE

TO THE

SIXTY-FOUR HEXAGRAMS

OF THE I CHING

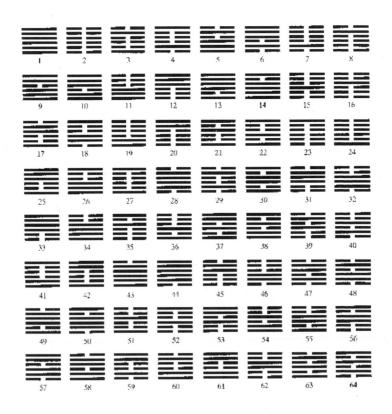

CHANGING LINES

1. The Power To Overcome

Now is a time of tremendous opportunity for initiating changes in yourself and your lifestyle. Because you are unusually well attuned to your deepest humanitarian and spiritual resources, you are now able to discover new meaning and direction in your life. Power and guidance will be available to overcome long standing inertia and to redirect the momentum of your understanding, attitudes, and habits. Grasp the fact that whatever you do now—even doing nothing—will have powerful consequences. Review your plans carefully. Know what to do and when to act as well as when not to act at all.

Your Resistance: Be prepared to challenge your usual beliefs about what you can't be or do. Beware being overwhelmed by the tyranny of the mundane and trivial which only strangle growth and preserve stagnation. Plan to be directed by your highest good rather than your usual impulses, fears, doubts, or resentments.

Your Next Step: Examine what is not working well in your life and what you can do to reform your habits and attitudes in order to bring more health and success into your life. Plan carefully what you want to happen, because it probably will. Ask only for what you want (in the long run) because you probably will get it and may regret it.

THE CHANGING LINES

6: The keynote is cautious optimism rather than being too idealistic. Take care to match your goals with your resources and opportunities.

5: Identify your highest good and go for it! This is a time to trust in your decisions and power.

4: Use this time to reform your immature and self-destructive habits rather than using your power to force others to do your will.

3: Don't be misdirected by old fears, doubts, desires, or the need to please others. Think for yourself and honor what is best for you.

2: Take time to define your ideals and recognize your heroes. Get to know them and draw inspiration from them.

1: Wait for a better time to act. Self-restraint is more useful to you than action now.

Unchanging: At all levels there are unparalleled opportunities to initiate reforms in your character and/or exert new directions in your self-expression. Seize the day, as you will find it progressively more difficult to do so later.

2. The Right Response

This is a time when you need to wake up and smell the coffee! Take stock of where you are and what has happened to you. By an honest review of your situation you can become aware of important signals and messages that you have been overlooking. Unclutter your thinking of old assumptions about being victimized, abandoned, hopeless, and powerless long enough to recognize the awesome truth about yourself. Learn to respond to the hidden message from your higher self in the patterns of your experiences.

Your Resistance: The greatest danger now is in being passive and subordinating yourself to inferior guidance by following the expectations of others or surrendering to your own fear, self-pity, and resentments. Seek to look beyond them to discover a new meaning and direction inherent in your struggles.

Your Next Step: Expand your perspective about your experiences to include the notion that adversity strengthens you and problems stimulate growth. Appreciate that you can probably do what many other people in your situation have been able to accomplish. Learn to follow their good example and methods.

THE CHANGING LINES

6: Check your motives and objectives as you may be trying to oppose the will and plan of your higher self. If so, you cannot win this struggle.

5: Instead of a direct assault on your problem, work to promote maturity and health directly by expanding your strengths, love, and skills.

4: Growth will be possible only if you can stay centered in your inner life and its potential for healing and enrichment.

3: Now is the time for modest and humble efforts to work on your own. Heroics will backfire and only attract the wrong kind of attention.

2: Get real! Your rationalizations, excuses, and defenses are showing. It's time to be honest about your responsibilities and strengths.

1: Your situation is deteriorating and you will need to adjust your plans and behavior accordingly.

Unchanging: It is vital that you do not succumb to defeatism and small-mindedness at this time. Discipline yourself to keep your eye on the goal. Draw strength from your higher self and the great abundance in the life around you.

3. Starting Over

There is an old saying that goes: "There are no failures or mistakes—only results!" And so if you do not like the results you are getting in your life, now is the time to make the necessary changes in your behavior to achieve better results. In this situation, it may be best to consider starting over again with a more enlightened sense of your identity, role, purpose, and objectives. Seek out these changes and accept them. Look for guidance in examples of success out of your past and the activities of others.

Your Resistance: Beware two major temptations: the tendency to work harder instead of smarter, and the habit of expecting to control every facet of your life. If you really knew what to do, you would be demonstrating that fact already.

Your Next Step: Review your priorities so as to be more realistic about your true needs and opportunities, then stick to them. Learn to tolerate some instability in your life. Out of this confusion can come room for an evolutionary change in your values and understanding. Be led by whatever insights you gain.

THE CHANGING LINES

6: Don't attempt to manage the present as you did in the past. You not only need new ways to think and act—you may need new values and motives.

5: Your situation is too unstable to do more than marshall all your resources and then use them very sparingly and skillfully.

4: It will be essential to humble yourself and learn to collaborate more effectively with your higher self.

3: You may be attempting to do more than is possible. Be realistic about your limitations and do not be misled by your stubbornness.

2: This situation is too confusing to do more than stay detached and hold your ground until clarity is possible.

1: The obstacle confronting you now is beyond your current ability to understand or resolve. Study it carefully as it can lead you to the inner life.

Unchanging: You suffer from a major blind spot about your beliefs, motives, and values. Until you accept the fact that it is these self-created factors which limit you, your progress will be blocked.

4. Blind Spots

You are being blinded by a lack of specific understanding or skills. This blind spot is so deep that you may not even understand what it is that you do not know, thereby creating this unusual level confusion and difficulty. It is essential to stop trying to resolve this situation in your usual way. You may need to search for more than just new techniques; you may need a whole new way of evaluating the issues and your role in it. Seek out advice and counsel from experts and your higher self. But take heart, this situation is in your life precisely in order to force you to learn.

Your Resistance: The insight you need right now may well challenge your major beliefs and values, bringing out your defensiveness and hostility to truth. Keep in mind that it is not you that is challenged—but only what you believe.

Your Next Step: Admit that the core of your problem lies in what you don't know and aren't doing. Then, be more willing to be flexible and learn what you need to—or suffer continued distress. Be ready to accept and apply answers, rather than just debate ideas.

THE CHANGING LINES

6: Your problem ultimately arises out of your own errors of omission and commission, and you will have to learn to solve it at this level.

5: Only by accepting this situation with humility can you open all the doors to learning what you need to resolve it.

4: Wise up! Your egotism and defenses are blinding you to the very truth that will free you.

3: If you insist in getting what you wish for now, you will be missing the meaning of this situation.

2: Remember that the weaknesses of human nature must be met with charity and skill—not anger.

1: You dishonor your potential by simply accepting yourself the way you are. Get busy!

Unchanging: This situation is an indirect result of a major blind spot about some defect in your values, habits, or lifestyle. The key to these issues lies in focusing on the learning you need rather than examining the suffering inherent in outer events.

5. Patience

This is a time of considerable change. Some confusion and instability may exist even in your own sense of what is right as well as your role in this situation. While events are in such a state of flux, it will be necessary to await further development before any clear solution can be formulated. Take this time to study and observe outer events and to refine your values, sense of purpose, and your habits. Above all, do not allow yourself to become unduly anxious or angry. You have no real control of this situation and must, instead, patiently endure it. Griping, blaming, and self-pity would be the worst of all possible choices to entertain at this time.

Your Resistance: Beware the temptation to be outraged at the delays, confusion, and your inability to take charge of this situation. Learn to accept gracefully what you cannot change or control at this time.

Your Next Step: Appreciate the need for patience now and how to cultivate this skill. This is not a passive or mentally numb state; instead, it is a matter of restraining your constructive skills and energies until the proper time.

THE CHANGING LINES

6: You will need to act soon. Be prepared to recognize hints and support from unusual sources.

5: Take this time to review your situation and renew your commitment to the work ahead for you.

4: You are at the very center of your difficulty. Stay calm and exercise restraint and caution.

3: Your situation makes you very vulnerable. Protect yourself by controlling fear and avoiding any kind of impulsive action.

2: What you intend doing may be controversial; if so, be prepared to deal with criticism.

1: Do not force a confrontation with problems as yet. Stay calm and wait for the situation to evolve.

Unchanging: This situation is beyond your conscious control or understanding at this time. Deeper meaning and patterns from your unconscious are emerging; these will eventually become clear. Only as you comprehend this situation more deeply will you be able to work your way out of it.

6. Disillusionment

The obstacle before you is substantial and undeniable. While you may believe that you understand your situation and your goal clearly, you are seeing only your own perspective. Your opposition also sees itself as correct, and therein lies a major conflict. It would be destructive to force the issue by aggressive attacks on your adversary. Likewise, the effort to devise clever plots to win will also backfire. Avoid disillusionment by rethinking your objectives as well as your motives. Seek counsel from neutral experts if necessary. Good fortune will come out of sincere efforts to compromise and to learn something from this experience.

Your Resistance: Pride in your own perspectives and values has blinded you to a larger view and context which can resolve this conflict. Fighting harder will not work in this situation.

Your Next Step: Review all your assumptions and expand your options before you defeat yourself in an unwinnable struggle. Stop attempting to validate what you already believe and instead seek out your highest good. Be ready to listen!

THE CHANGING LINES

6: Aggressive action now to attack this problem will only perpetuate it. Look beyond the conflict to discover the clue to harmony and growth.

5: You need to collaborate with your higher self more effectively. Seek its counsel and follow it this time.

4: You may be permitting minor annoyances to disturb you more than it's worth. Honor your dignity more than your pride in this situation.

3: Abandon any righteous attitudes. Spend your energy building harmony rather than walls.

2: It is time to stop fighting every battle that comes your way. Accept this situation as is and put your energy into more constructive efforts.

1: Just focus on surviving this situation now in order to preserve what little you have.

Unchanging: The universe is challenging some of your most important assumptions and you will be forced to yield. Remember, it is not you that is being defeated here but your own rigidity and erroneous beliefs.

Your authority in this situation is weak, and there is a risk that your independent or unorthodox action now will backfire. The reason for this is that the situation you are confronting has it roots either in the negative qualities in your unconscious or the negativity in the collective beliefs and habits of many people close to you. It will be important to proceed with tact to avoid offending or challenging either the public or your own unconscious forces. Instead, good fortune will come from seeking to align yourself with the highest good for all of you and then working quietly to establish this.

Your Resistance: Avoid the temptation to just reject your own strong feelings or those close to you, no matter how negative. You cannot afford to shock or alienate those near you or even strongly oppose your old habits and attitudes.

Your Next Step: Discipline yourself to cultivate greater harmony with your own nature and to be charitable about others. Progress will come step by step and with the support of others, including your unconscious. Seek to bring everything together under a higher purpose that serves your mutual interests.

THE CHANGING LINES

6: Recognize the difference between being led by the constructive elements in your life versus just attempting to defeat the negative.

5: Do not trust your feelings now. Follow the counsel of a wise person or your higher self.

4: You cannot win this struggle. Plan a strategic retreat and regroup your forces to go around it.

3: Your focus is too superficial. Seek a larger view and purpose in your endeavor.

2: You need to drop your defensiveness and participate in meaningful discussions with your higher self and others.

1: Avoid radical or impulsive actions. Your success now depends on thoughtful analysis and disciplined behavior.

Unchanging: You have allowed yourself to become too focused on your personal needs and wants. Consequently, you may have become estranged from your higher self and the noble elements of all humanity. Strive to appreciate that ultimately we all strive for the same goals and that we need each other's help.

8. A New View

You need to examine the larger context of your situation. You may have become partially blinded by being so close to the problem that you are unwilling or unable to recognize the deeper roots and complexity of it. Social traditions as well as your misguided assumptions may have misled you into a narrow perspective that is blocking your progress now. You need a new view that incorporates the life and vision of your higher self. It will be essential to look beyond your personal self-interest and seek out what would be the highest good for everyone involved in this situation. Prepare yourself to entertain new directions and roles that might require some sacrifice on your part.

Your Resistance: Beware the easy temptation of allowing your desire for personal comfort or isolation to direct your decisions and behavior. If you insist on practicing exclusion, you will be ignored.

Your Next Step: You are being called to look at your situation from a more inclusive perspective and to embrace a new degree of harmony with others as well as with your higher self.

THE CHANGING LINES

6: Your interpretation of events is deficient because it is too self-serving. Try for greater harmony with all parties involved.

5: Your world is full of an abundance of opportunities and resources to grow and be helpful. Stop ignoring them and seize them now.

4: The bond with your higher self is strong and active now. Let it inspire you as you review your priorities and refresh your attitudes.

3: You may have aligned yourself to assumptions, traditions, or a group that is inferior. Begin again and seek a higher quality.

2: Be careful or you may be misled by popular sentiment or your own desires. Good fortune will come from honoring your principles.

1: A simple attitude of goodwill and a humble desire to be helpful will do more to align you to what is right than anything else.

Unchanging: You may have become stuck in your own narrow perspective and assumptions until all you see is your own projections and rationalizations. You need to examine how others and your higher self might see your situation.

9. Limitation

This is a time to appreciate the limits of your authority and power since you have very little influence in this situation. An aggressive style of confrontation now would guarantee a disaster. Any effort to impose your will on this matter will lead to self-destruction. Your best course will be to practice good diplomacy and patient cooperation. You will need all your charm and skill to finesse this situation. Work on cultivating those qualities of character that produce harmony, tolerance, and a capacity to preserve your dignity while staying centered in your principles. If this is impossible, the best course may be to withdraw entirely until a better time.

Your Resistance: Your rigidity, impatience, and inability to compromise is being challenged. Now is a time for more skill and grace under pressure—rather than more assertiveness.

Your Next Step: Carefully assess the limitations of your authority and opportunities and then work out a plan and style that is a model of patience and self-restraint.

THE CHANGING LINES

6: Appreciate what advantage you have and the progress made. Do not pursue this matter further or you may lose what you have.

5: Don't try to work in isolation. Seek the help of those with whom you can share both resources and benefits.

4: You may need to overcome self-deception and abandon excuses to find a better way out of this situation.

3: Do not assume that things are as calm or as simple as they appear, because you still have some lessons to learn from this situation.

2: The unconscious roots and power of this situation are stronger than you realize. Go easy or you may be overwhelmed.

1: Study this situation more carefully. There are deeper patterns and issues at play which will require great skill to manage.

Unchanging: Your situation is relatively fixed and you will be forced to accommodate it as it is presently structured. Your challenge will be to practice self-restraint and to refine your motives, desires, and style.

10. Balance

In changing times, there is always a need to balance our desires with our needs and duties. This is such a time, and you are being called to reexamine your values, motives, and goals. The great area of conflict will be between surface feelings and your deeper values, between your habitual responses and what is more appropriate in this situation. Impulsiveness, strong reactions, and egotism will produce a strong backlash now. The situation requires that you center yourself in your principles while adopting a tone of generosity and optimism in what you say and do. Do not be defensive, but also do not be a doormat. Redefine the nature of your highest good and then honor it with as much grace and courage as possible.

Your Resistance: You may be too caught up in egotism, pettiness, or old unresolved conflicts to appreciate the reality of this situation. Don't let these issues blind you to honoring your long term interests and progress.

Your Next Step: Recognize where you are being misled by your feelings and assumptions and put aside old resentments and desires. Seek out the good potential of this situation and be guided solely by the effort to develop it.

THE CHANGING LINES

6: By examining the record of your achievements and failures, you can recognize what your higher self has been supporting or discouraging.

5: Your situation is unstable and you risk disappointment unless you protect yourself with a good plan and the steady determination to achieve.

4: Be attentive and flexible. You will be successful only to the degree that you notice the hints and clues that will guide you along the way.

3: You may be trying to accomplish too much. If you force the issue, unconscious patterns may push back with greater power and unpleasant results.

2: To be successful, you must keep a low profile and very modest expectations. Restrain unrealistic enthusiasm as well as fears.

1: Because your power is limited, keep your goals and style as modest as possible. Neither expect or promise too much to others.

Unchanging: You may be somewhat lost in a fog of narrow expectations or simply be too passive in the naïve hope that things will turn out well. You need to pay more attention to defining and promoting the highest good in this situation and in disciplining your tendency to let the superficial control you.

11. Growth

At the beginning of any situation, there is a moment of inspiration and hope which carries us into the first few steps. At these times, we can sense a definite rapport with higher forces as well as the work at hand. In fact, there is unusual harmony between the personality and the higher self. Consequently, we will sense an awakening of new courage, confidence, and inner peace. Use this time to expand your ability to make sense of problems, to grasp new insights about yourself and your situation in life, begin new projects, and heal relationships.

Your Resistance: A deeply tranquil mood at this time may lull you into relaxing rather than using this opportunity for soul searching, healing, and improving your attunement to the higher self.

Your Next Step: Now is the time to work at dissolving barriers and building bridges of goodwill wherever there is disharmony or unhealthy divisions in your life.

THE CHANGING LINES

6: It will be best to focus on improving good relationships and activities rather than trying to repair those which are not working.

5: Do not allow tranquility to turn into euphoria and egotism. You will receive more respect and trust if you set a modest style and attitude.

4: You can make significant progress now if you trust in your higher self and follow your spiritual principles.

3: Guard your faith in yourself! Challenging times are best managed by a firm conviction in your own abilities and powers to survive.

2: Do not be misled by temptation or fads. Keep your eye on your long term goals. Be kind to people whom you may need later on.

1: Charitable attitudes and activities will be unusually successful now and will attract favorable attention and alliances.

Unchanging: There is an unusual mood of harmony within you as well as with your higher self. Seek and trust your inner guidance and use these insights for self-healing, renewal, and enrichment.

12. Impasse

The interests of your personality seem to be directly opposed to your higher self and, therefore, higher forces are not available to assist in many outer activities. This is a time when there may be much frustration in your efforts to heal the wounds of the personality or to grow beyond its limits. Likewise, this period may seriously test your faith and patience to endure. It is important to view this apparent state of impasse as temporary rather that permanent. Do not leap to conclusions that your situation is cursed or doomed. Hold fast to your ideals and keep faith in the worthiness of your aims.

Your Resistance: There may be a strong temptation to give up entirely or to resort to inferior methods of promoting well-being such as blaming others, denying problems, expressing anger, or behaving selfishly.

Your Next Step: Review your innermost purpose and values. Recommit yourself to these ideals despite current events. Draw on the strength of these convictions to help you endure the frustration of difficult times.

THE CHANGING LINES

6: Your best course of action will require your determination to stay committed to your highest good. Your real enemy is your own hesitation.

5: Fundamental healing is possible if you lay the groundwork for it now, rather than pursue quick results.

4: Do not stimulate resistance by imposing radical new demands on yourself or others. Seek harmony and consensus rather than outright control.

3: You have allowed inferior beliefs to lead you into activities which dishonor your highest good and needs. Withdraw and rethink your motives.

2: Do not compromise your integrity just to feel good or get along with others. Be ready to recognize and deal with temptation for what it is.

1: Your individuality and honor are being tested. If you must, withdraw from situations or plans which are inferior.

Unchanging: There is a major hindrance that blocks the direct resolution of this situation. Look for a more cosmic reason why this blockage exists. You may need to seek alternate goals and plans or just work to accept gracefully current matters.

13. Integration

There are times when independent action is called for, but this is not one of them. Now is a time when you must consider your place in a multitude of diverse interests, impulses, goals, and desires. This is a time for putting your mental household in order, for ending internal conflicts and for healing ambivalence, doubts, and double standards. It may be that some of your wants conflict with your needs or that your desires for immediate gratification conflict with your highest good. Therefore, it will be important to integrate your various goals, desires, convictions, and motives around your most important aims in life.

Your Resistance: Beware the easy temptation to hesitate and procrastinate as a way to avoid a confrontation with the issues and internal conflicts that demand a decision by you right now.

Your Next Step: You need to review your long term goals and bring your priorities into harmony with them. This step will help you stop dividing your energies and, sometimes, sabotaging your success.

THE CHANGING LINES

6: Only superficial harmony exists in this situation, so do not depend on it to support major changes.

5: Communicate your needs more overtly with your opposition, and you may find that you share some common goals and can work cooperatively after all.

4: This is not the time to be too independent, because this will separate you from those forces or people you need to succeed.

3: You are working against parts of yourself or others that oppose your overt goals. Realign your activities before mutual antagonism destroys all.

2: Beware the tendency to allow self-interest to separate you from your higher self and its purpose. Rethink your goals and methods.

1: You can harness all your forces if you pursue your primary need rather than the diverse wishes and wants of your subconscious.

Unchanging: Your success depends on identifying and learning the lessons you need. This will bring benefit to every part of your character and endeavors.

14. Good Fortune

An aura of success touches everything you do now. These are fortunate times for you—if you know what is good for you. There are hidden reserves of inner strength and good fortune in outer activities to help you achieve your goals. Unhappily, these times can also tempt you to fall into the trap of egotism and selfishness. Only modesty and humility can help you preserve your balance and avoid the risk of pride or of evoking jealousy and opposition from others. Align your good fortune to your ideals and your principles.

Your Resistance: Excessive confidence and egotism can lead you to neglect your highest good in favor of simple vanity and what feels good. Take care to be realistic and fair in managing your problems and opportunities.

Your Next Step: Review your principles and goals to be sure they reflect your highest good. Seek the larger view of your higher self and act with integrity; good fortune will follow.

THE CHANGING LINES

6: Great success is possible as long as you respect the power and direction of the higher self in all that you do.

5: Maintain a mature tone in all your relationships including the one with your higher self. Getting too personal will weaken your position.

4: Concentrate on what you need to do rather than being distracted by your fears, doubts, or the activities and opinions of others.

3: You need more support from your higher self, and you can receive it by a sincere rededication to its purpose and plan.

2: Success will come from using your faith, skill, and cunning to magnify your strengths and opportunities.

1: The first few steps may seem too easy, and perhaps they are. Beware; hidden obstacles may surface. Exercise caution and be safe.

Unchanging: You have great power to achieve your goals if you retain a simple agenda, a modest style, and a firm adherence to your principles. Your greatest threat comes from your own arrogance and inflexibility.

15. Being Centered

Life is full of extremes of both triumphs and failures. If we become excessively concerned with either extreme, dominated by foolish enthusiasm or desperate frustration, we will find that life goes on without us. It is vital to remain centered in our mature strengths and principles to grasp our true identity and what we need to do. It is as important to avoid overconfidence as it is to avoid apathy. Naïve faith can be just as fatal as neurotic doubt and alienation. Now is a time to stay centered in sincere but moderate attitudes and beliefs. This will protect you from excessive caution as well as excessive enthusiasm.

Your Resistance: Beware acting on impulse or having unrealistic expectations. Your impatience may tempt you to give up too soon or take on too much responsibility.

Your Next Step: Patience and temperance should be the keynotes of your thoughts and behavior. Modest expectations and humble but methodical efforts will guarantee steady success.

THE CHANGING LINES

6: Look first at how to help yourself. Healing can come as much from self-restraint as from new benevolent thoughts and behavior.

5: If you stay centered and act in moderation, it will help you to focus your determination and be persistent in what you need to do now.

4: One battle won does not end the conflict. You need to be consistent in your efforts to stay centered and act responsibly.

3: Do not allow self-discipline to weaken. Beware the temptation to relax too much or to indulge in blaming, self-pity, or fanatical pursuits.

2: Mature self-control precedes your control of outer situations. This, in turn, will evoke support from your higher self.

1: Be careful. Your overconfidence, resentment, or passivity will attract opposition from your unconscious as well as from without.

Unchanging: You need to walk a careful middle path between all extremes of advice and emotions, whether your own or others. Success comes through patience and persistent determination to honor your principles.

16. Divine Order

Each of us is born with an internal spiritual design and purpose which we are eventually expected to fulfill in our outer behavior. The will of spirit as well as the order of divine law supports these healing and evolutionary changes. Now is a time when you need to appreciate and honor divine order in your life and in the conduct of your affairs. More specifically, you need to focus on the agenda of your higher self and the internal order that already exists at this level. By bringing your personal values, beliefs, and actions into harmony with this internal order, much growth and healing is possible.

Your Resistance: The status quo always seems to defend itself, no matter how bad it is. Beware of old habits of allowing physical appetites, assumptions, and social traditions to deceive you.

Your Next Step: Seek a more enlightened redefinition of your sense of purpose and what is most important for you as a way of making deep and powerful healing changes in your situation and behavior.

THE CHANGING LINES

6: You may be caught somewhere in the past. Update your goals and priorities to be more responsive to current opportunities.

5: Do not succumb to frustration by trying to control the uncontrollable. If partial success is all you can achieve, then go for that.

4: Your own quiet faith and steady devotion to your goals will evoke the support of higher forces and friends who can help you.

3: You have become too passive. Trust your common sense. Use the best ideas you have and get to work.

2: Discipline of your attention and efforts to avoid the temptation to revert to old beliefs and habits or faddish nonsense.

1: Strong devotion to your higher self and belief in the worthiness of your goals are not enough. You must also work very diligently.

Unchanging: It is imperative that your ambivalence and internal conflicts be resolved in favor of a new commitment to honoring your highest good. By a sincere sacrifice to this purpose, internal harmony is achieved and progress assured.

17. Accepting

There are times when you need to assert yourself and other times when you need to accept things as they are by adapting to existing situations. This does not mean passive self-rejection or slavish obedience. It means that it is unwise to oppose the deeper and more established current trends. Your highest good will be served by making the best of your situation. This requires that you take an active role in skillfully managing your immediate circumstances. It is vital that you work in alliance with the realities about you rather than in opposition to them. Confident pragmatism will work better for you than naïve idealism or angry defensiveness.

Your Resistance: You may be tempted to resist reality or reject your duty in coping with this situation—or just aggressively impose your will. All of these choices will lead to great frustration.

Your Next Step: Accept the reality of your situation and "take up your cross." Recognize your role and duty in being an agent for the plans of your higher self. Discipline your personal wants and wishes as necessary to sustain this effort.

THE CHANGING LINES

6: You already know enough to take charge of this situation. If you act impersonally, higher forces will help you.

5: Your idealism, if applied with sincere commitment and practical action, will be a correct path.

4: Do not be tempted to follow inferior choices that produce only temporary relief through escape, denial, or self-deception.

3: Your correct path may lead you away from familiar beliefs, habits, and rituals. Prepare to look for new and better substitutes.

2: To make room for help from your higher self you will need to do some thorough soul searching and mental housecleaning.

1: Your situation is evolving or has changed since you evaluated it. You need to broaden your views and reexamine all of your options. You may have prematurely excluded wise choices.

Unchanging: This is not the time to be a visionary. You must begin by accepting and managing this situation as it exists right now rather than what you hope it will become. Realize that nothing will change until you assume your responsibility to take the first few steps.

18. Reform

There are times when a situation has deteriorated to such a point that we are ready to say, "What a mess!" Despite our good intentions and lofty plans, something is decidedly wrong about the object of your inquiry. Study this situation from every angle to understand why it has become so unworkable. It may be that you have been living in a naive dream world of idealism instead of practical action. Or you may have been focusing on analysis instead of work. Perhaps you have sought to manage this situation by looking for reasons why you have no responsibility to fix things. Whatever it is, it is obvious that you have neglected the practical and constructive activities which are needed now to improve matters.

Your Resistance: Beware the temptation to be combative, to sulk in apathy, or to try to substitute positive thought for positive action.

Your Next Step: Be pragmatic. Instead of reformulating long range goals or shuffling your values, just focus on the few, practical, and simple constructive activities that you can perform now.

THE CHANGING LINES

6: Your guide to correct action lies in being detached from problems and more attentive to your spiritual values.

5: Seek first to reform some of your habits and attitudes. Higher forces and others will support these changes.

4: If you don't take some positive action, things will just get worse. Be more involved, but in a constructive way.

3: Despite the internal voices of fear, doubt, or anger, you have good ideas for intervening to reform this situation. Act now.

2: You need to reform your most fundamental values and priorities. These changes will be revolutionary and affect everything in you.

1: This deteriorating situation is caused by the fact that you are clinging to outworn convictions and habits. Loosen up!

Unchanging: You may have meticulous plans, lofty goals, and sterling principles, but you also need determined action to demonstrate them. Do more to "walk what you talk."

19. Self-Realization

There is an unusual state of rapport with your higher self and its energies. Use this time to reflect on the meaning of whatever has challenged you. Recall your hopes, dreams, and ideals as a basis for gaining new insights into them. You will be able to make sense of your situation and see where you are headed. Perhaps you will feel more connected to spirit and with others on the path to enlightenment. Or you may just sense a renewal or new peak of confidence and joy about your world. Look for these changes and seek to ground them in your character by reforming and fine-tuning your values, sense of identity, and your view of the world.

Your Resistance: Your allegiance to habits of apathy, doubt and blaming may cause you to reject your potential for optimism, confidence, and goodwill. Don't be a cynic!

Your Next Step: Take more time for inner study and contemplation of meaning in your life. Review your values, attitudes, and beliefs. Mental housecleaning will never be more possible or useful for you than now.

THE CHANGING LINES

6: Now is the time to be gentle and encouraging to others or those aspects of your personality that need your wisdom and expertise.

5: You have good values and goals, but need to avoid the temptation to do everything yourself, lest you interfere with forces from your higher self.

4: You are on the correct path. Keep faith in the worthiness of your goals despite some apparent resistance.

3: There is danger in becoming too complacent or hopeful. You are on the correct path, but proceed with caution.

2: Your close attunement with your higher self on this matter will magnify your efforts and impel you toward success. Don't change your plans.

1: If you have defined worthwhile goals, you can be assured of support from higher forces and friends on your wavelength. Seek them out.

Unchanging: Old ideals and hopes now come to life and can be used very effectively for internal reform, self-healing, and charitable action. Seize the moment to inaugurate inner changes and useful action.

20. Inner Patterns

If we want to find the best course of action to take, we must first know where we are and where we have come from as a child of God as well as a child of earth. By understanding the inner patterns and forces that lie behind our current situation, we also recognize the real need for help or reform. By understanding how this situation has evolved, we recognize the innate pattern and momentum which are now unfolding. These insights reveal the natural patterns and laws that govern the subject of your inquiry. Knowing these things will prepare you to act wisely and work in harmony with divine law and higher forces.

Your Resistance: A superficial examination of this situation will likely mislead you. Blaming others or inventing slick, popular explanations will not work here. A complete overhaul of your thinking is needed.

Your Next Step: Study the situation more deeply for effective answers. Be more involved in it. Observe it more closely. Get beneath the surface of events and statements to look for ways of improving basic communication, attitudes, beliefs, and harmony.

THE CHANGING LINES

6: Detachment will be required to open the door to the insights you need about this situation.

5: The answer lies in examining how you can help others. Your good example may be controversial, but you will be correct.

4: Be guided by the examples of enlightened people, groups, and how they manage situations similar to yours.

3: You need a more realistic appraisal of your situation. Look at the results you are getting rather than your expectations and assumptions.

2: Your viewpoint suffers from toxic self-absorption. Seek a view that is more inclusive of others and your highest good.

1: Your sense of proportion is warped by a concern for your own comfort. Seek a more enlightened perspective.

Unchanging: Do not attempt to resolve this situation until you have thoroughly studied it from all angles. Seek alignment with the divine laws and their evolutionary momentum governing the inner patterns of these issues. Once you understand this, you will be able to be effective in mastering it.

21. Inner Conflict

When two incompatible forces meet, the result is great conflict, disorder, and ultimately, destruction. Such is the nature of this situation. This time, the real battle is within you. It is between the will and design of your higher self and the apathy, illusions, misconceptions, and false beliefs in your character. The higher forces will eventually win out even if it must be done at the expense of your discomfort. It is urgent that you take a fearless inventory of your values, beliefs, and habits to see what works for you and what doesn't. By reviewing everything to determine if it serves your highest good, the essential reforms you need can be made in time to avert disaster.

Your Resistance: You may have been "going with the flow" so long that you have drifted into the chaos of meaningless self-serving illusions. Stop consulting your fears, fantasies, or anger for advice and get to work on genuine solutions.

Your Next Step: Take time to define your most important objectives and priorities. Clear out fuzzy ideas, the clutter of lazy thinking, and simplistic excuses. Frustration and stalemate will continue until you consult and cooperate with the direction of your higher self.

THE CHANGING LINES

6: Unless you regain a better sense of purpose and direction, chaos will surround you.

5: Lacking a perfect or comfortable solution, you must pick the best of current alternatives and apply all your determination to its execution.

4: Even though immense work lies ahead of you, success can be achieved by unwavering determination to do what you can each moment.

3: It is more important to work so as to honor your principles than it is to get quick results. Keep faith in the worthiness of your goal.

2: What goes around comes around. This may be unpleasant, but it will lead to long overdue reforms and revisions of habits.

1: You are being nudged to notice your mistakes in choices and behavior. Heed this warning now before your error is compounded.

Unchanging: Major conflict within your own conscience and emotions is unavoidable. It will be essential to make a radical reform of your beliefs and habits. This will be unpleasant and painful, but it will clear the path for a major breakthrough to more enlightened living.

22. Perfection

Sometimes in a wonderful moment of clarity, we sense the hidden perfection behind all events. We feel a peaceful communion with the infinite. Everything seems to be in harmony and we are one with that harmony. These moments can be brief, but exhilarating. They also can be deceptive in that—while they are real—they will not last, because this harmony is based on subjective feeling and pure idealism more than reality. What is felt may not be attainable and, in fact, may mislead us if we try to base our plans on it. While you may have glimpsed divine perfection, your real work will be to manifest it. Beware this difference and be practical.

Your Resistance: Your illusions and positive fantasies may lull your rational faculties into confusing idealistic possibilities with practical realities. Keep egotism in check. Your judgment may be distorted by transient euphoric feelings.

Your Next Step: Enjoy these tranquil moments. Recognize your inspiration as revealing long term divine possibilities. Use them to refine your values and grasp of the larger picture, but restrain euphoric and idealistic urges to make radical changes in your plans or style now.

THE CHANGING LINES

6: Let your cheerfulness and benevolence shine through you without restriction. Your genuine charm will produce astounding results.

5: To increase your rapport with others and your higher self, be guided by your good intentions and sincere affection rather than clever schemes.

4: To tap your divine possibilities, restrain your flamboyance in favor of being authentic and humble.

3: It is important to keep up a steady flow of practical effort even when we feel a strong inner confidence and optimism.

2: Do not allow grandiose feelings and illusions to control you. Concentrate on the feasible.

1: It is vital to focus on what is workable and within reach. There is no easy shortcut to your goal.

Unchanging: There is unusual harmony in your current affairs and you can glimpse the latent divinity of yourself and this situation. But beware that you can be blinded by a perfection that exists only at an inner level. This may have little connection with outer reality as yet.

23. Restraint

Your position is weak and there may be little you can do other than practice restraint until times change. Inferior elements in your situation seem to be in control of matters, and your interests and needs are being ignored. If you try to combat these trends, you will only increase your frustration and foster opposition. Now is a time for you to take on full responsibility for caring for your needs. Expect little from others. Work at sustaining a tranquil and dignified attitude about everything, including your enemies as well as your problems. Eventually, others will respect you for your self-restraint and calmness in times of distress.

Your Resistance: Restrain your natural instinct to fix this situation by the clever use of your wits and skill. Also restrain your impatience and resentment about what you cannot control.

Your Next Step: Be mindful of your limited power and role in this situation. Strive for a gracious and benevolent attitude but have limited expectations. Your dignified behavior will be an excellent investment in subsequent developments.

THE CHANGING LINES

6: Be patient. Your authority and influence will soon rise as the cycle is shifting to favor superior ideas and talent.

5: The forces against you are weakening. If you solicit cooperation with higher forces and friends, you can be successful.

4: A crisis is building, and you may be unable to avoid it. Avoid defensive maneuvers but hold fast to your principles.

3: Your situation may be difficult, but if you let your higher principles guide you, you will know what to do and can endure without fault or damage.

2: You will need to adjust quietly to this situation. Combative attitudes or maneuvers will backfire on you.

1: You are opposed by forces or people who do not respect your best interests. Strive for great caution and patience rather than forceful action.

Unchanging: You have no significant ability to influence this situation. Be calm and accept what you cannot change. Maintain a gracious attitude and demonstrate kindness where possible, but restrain the urge to take charge. By accepting these situations, you preserve your strength for better times.

24. Cycles

This is a time in life when events seem to be saying to you, "Hello again." Certain familiar cycles of opportunity or challenges are now recurring. Some things are being phased out while other opportunities are coming into your affairs. It may be that something that has blocked you is now passing out of your life, or that you will experience a breakthrough in overcoming some internal hindrance such as persistent fear, doubt, or resentment. It is important to recognize these cyclic patterns in your life, because they provide key insights into your spiritual lessons and how to cope with them. How you have managed these cycles of opportunity in the past will provide profound clues to your next step.

Your Resistance: Restrain both your apathy and your impatience. Apathy and doubt may have so blinded you that you may not be able to recognize good opportunity in time to seize it. Your impatience to push ahead now may prematurely sabotage healthy beginnings.

Your Next Step: Recognize that this situation represents a recurring pattern of events for you. Study what you have and have not yet learned from your previous exposures to these cycles. Revise your attitudes and habits in light of these learnings.

THE CHANGING LINES

6: Hesitation or stubbornness may have caused you to wait too long to act and your opportunity may be lost.

5: Review your beliefs and reasoning about this situation. Change yourself before you act this time.

4: You may have to proceed without the support of friends. Despite a few doubts, trust your judgment and act accordingly.

3: Try to dispel the mental fog created by your own anxieties and speculation and go with the best ideas you have.

2: Be encouraged by the success of others in similar situations. Solicit the support of your higher self. This will ensure success.

1: You may be enticed to act selfishly. You will gain a larger victory by sticking to your values and principles.

Unchanging: Each person bears a unique set of patterns for lessons to learn and opportunities to serve. Recognize them as the cause of having attracted certain situations into your life. They are inevitable. Accept them with serenity and wisdom.

25. Humility

Sometimes we are humbled by the many unexpected obstacles and delays that we encounter on our path. It seems as if there is no direct route to our goal. This describes the situation of your inquiry. Despite meticulous planning and reasoned judgments, you may encounter many surprises and hindrances. Your best course of action will be to flow with events and allow your highest intuition and principles to guide you spontaneously. Permit the wisdom of your superconscious mind to take over and automatically direct your decisions and activity. This action permits the emergence of serendipity, which will be more valuable to you than logic at this time.

Your Resistance: Do not allow annoyance to energize your frustration or sabotage what you can do. Recognize that you are trying to control the uncontrollable right now. Correct your attitude and restrain your combative approach.

Your Next Step: There is an inner wisdom in this situation which governs its unfoldment. Be more open to letting your creative intuition guide what you do. Now is the time to trust your hunches more than logic. Only a humble approach will be successful.

THE CHANGING LINES

6: Your only influence on this situation right now would be to make it worse. It is best to do nothing at all.

5: What is perceived as a problem is actually an internal cleansing process which is exposing old patterns. Do not obstruct this basic process.

4: Traditional answers and logical advice may mislead you. Seek and follow an inner, intuitive guidance.

3: Bad things still happen to good people. Try to view your challenges with as much humility and creativity as possible.

2: Concentrate only on managing the immediate situation, because you do not understand the inner patterns that govern the outcome of this matter.

1: By being centered in your devotion and commitment to your principles, you can be certain that your course of action will be correct.

Unchanging: Prepare for surprises, for this situation will be full of the unexpected. Plan to be flexible, creative, and adaptable to these changes. Your own stubborrnness and rigid expectations will be your worst enemy.

26. Inner Power

There is an unusual alignment with your higher self and its power to influence you. Because of this, anything you do now is likely to be enhanced with unusual force that may overwhelm you and others. It will be wise to carefully consider your moves, because your slightest gesture may produce a major response. Seek guidance from all that you have learned from your experiences as well as the wisdom of others. Your influence on others will be potent. While this can greatly enhance your capacity to communicate and draw individuals to you, be extremely considerate of how your speech and behavior will affect others.

Your Resistance: Do not attempt to use this extra power for largely selfish purposes or to oppose traditions, because this may provoke an explosion. Beware the temptation to become over-confident and attempt impulsive or aggressive moves.

Your Next Step: Review your beliefs and goals in light of your experience and the current situation. Look for fresh insights into the meaning of these events as well as the nature of your highest good. Then act promptly with wisdom and great self-control.

THE CHANGING LINES

6: Only if you follow the path to your highest good will you accomplish much. Seek guidance.
5: Use all your energies to serve noble purposes. Redirect negative impulses by harnessing them to higher motives and values.
4: Delays may have held you back, but the determination and skills you now need are stronger than ever.
3: Success is likely if you stay focused on your highest good and do not allow distractions.
2: Hold your ground quietly but do not attempt to push ahead or you may provoke trouble for yourself.
1: The forces opposing you are powerful. You would be wise to restrain yourself and simply appreciate what you have.

Unchanging: You have unusual power for self-expression; therefore, plan carefully and act with great self-restraint. Seek the support of your higher self and its direction before you act. If inner guidance is not clear, follow traditions or the example of leaders you trust.

27. Investing

What we sow, we also reap. The quality of our motives and attitudes are potent forces that we all invest in our daily activities. If we nurse grudges, we feed our resentments and build hostility. If we give praise and feel gratitude for worthwhile events, we build goodwill and joy. It is important to view current events with this principle in mind. In fact, we can measure the quality of our beliefs and expectations by the results we are getting, for there is now a very strong connection between the two. If our situation is disappointing, we should look at what we are investing in it. Take heed and act appropriately.

Your Resistance: Avoid the temptation to explain stalemate, failures, or other problems by rounding up the usual suspects of helplessness or blaming others. Don't just analyze what is wrong or how others have failed you. Seek to discover what you can do to help yourself.

Your Next Step: It is time to consider how this situation mirrors what you have done or left undone. Accept full responsibility for improving matters. Aim higher so as to reconnect with issues and people on a more constructive wavelength.

THE CHANGING LINES

6: Avoid dreamy or theoretical speculation. Focus strictly on what is the best you can achieve in spite of the limits of this situation.

5: Your constructive intentions will fail unless you work with your higher self to manage the unconscious aspects of this problem.

4: Charitable activities will now be successful, especially if you ally yourself with others who seek to do the same.

3: Stop looking for sympathy or someone to blame. You really need to face the truth about the constructive things you can do.

2: You can increase your power and opportunities by doing more to take care of your own needs. At present, you risk becoming too dependent.

1: Your idealism, jealousy, or tendency to imitate others is distorting what is appropriate for you. Work to discover and pursue your own needs.

Unchanging: The results you are getting are in direct relation to the quality of your attitudes and behavior. Examine all your responses to what challenges you. Any excessive concern about the dark side of life will only feed negativity. Be more constructive and less reactive.

28. Crisis

Many trends and forces are closing in on you at the same time. Perhaps there are unusual demands being placed on you. Or perhaps you are simply caught in the middle of conflicting forces and chaotic events. In any case, your situation now is quite unstable, and it will be essential for you to have a plan of action to cope with matters. Do not hesitate except to review your options. Do not attempt to straddle the issues or avoid your responsibility. You must make a decision and stand by it or you can be swept away in the confusion. If necessary, be ready to withdraw totally. Absolute commitment and steadfastness will be necessary. This is a test of your character, so do not let yourself down.

Your Resistance: Don't try to deny the issues or your need to play a decisive role in them. Do not attempt to go with the flow or allow panic, resentment, self-pity, or other reactions to rule you. Instead, seek your inner guidance.

Your Next Step: Consult with your innermost goals and values. Try to see this situation from the view of your higher self. Is there a lesson or divine principle that is being demonstrated? Once you discern the higher significance of it, make your decision and stand by it.

THE CHANGING LINES

6: Worthwhile objectives may require a huge effort and sacrifice. Still, this can be the correct choice.

5: You must be realistic in evaluating your resources for achieving your goals. Avoid naive hope and fuzzy idealism now.

4: Seek your own counsel about what you can or cannot do and be aware that this is a powerful time for you.

3: Stubborn persistence in clinging to old habits and desires is your weakest point. You need to rethink your goals and be more flexible.

2: Draw support and comfort from others who are struggling with a similar challenge.

1: Be attentive to all nuances in this situation. Plan carefully, because any action now may have considerable consequences.

Unchanging: Events and forces around you are overwhelming. You will need to cut back on your activities and streamline your goals to fit the time and the resources you have. Absolute self-reliance is essential to making the correct decisions. Do not delay this evaluation.

29. Challenge

Life is full of challenges, and the subject of your inquiry is another hurdle for you to manage. The source of this lies in your external environment rather than in some aberration of your beliefs or habits. Nevertheless the challenge presents a test of your character and will. It will not be possible to avoid this confrontation without loss. A simple truce would only result in loss of your momentum. It is imperative to meet this challenge with all your strength and skill. Success comes through firm adherence to your principles and ethics. It is essential that you do not compromise yourself at any point.

Your Resistance: Do not allow fear, anger, or confusion to control you. So also, do not attempt to avoid this challenge or bargain your way out of it. Your firm action is required; do not shirk from it.

Your Next Step: Look for new understanding of the risks about you and the character of others involved in this situation. Carefully choose your policy and what you will and will not tolerate. If your standards cannot be met, you may need to withdraw from this challenge if that is possible.

THE CHANGING LINES

6: All your clever efforts seem blocked, and the situation may be at a stalemate. Hold steady and wait for better times.

5: There is danger that aggressive action will provoke more trouble. Limit yourself to small, gentle, effective moves.

4: Do not try to bluff others or otherwise be manipulative. Modest, uncomplicated plans and action will serve you best.

3: Unless you are exceptionally certain of what to do, do nothing until you have more information about this situation.

2: Be realistic about your position in this matter. A reasonable goal would be to manage the situation as best you can to survive.

1: You have lowered your standards and expectations too far and compromised your principles. It will be necessary to begin again.

Unchanging: There is a pattern to this kind of challenge, and you need to look at why you are so vulnerable to its recurrence. Success comes through your dedication to a more constructive attitude and skillful response to it.

30. Collaboration

Sometimes success at a material level requires the collaborative efforts of many people. So also, success in personal growth and self-healing may require collaboration with others as well as with our higher self. Often, this cooperation must begin within the diverse parts of our character or the various roles we play. It will be important to strive for harmony among these elements as well as with higher forces. The focus of this integration may be a common purpose or common role. Or it could be a common goal or principle or a spiritual law that draws you together. Find that point and seek to harmonize your interests and activities about it.

Your Resistance: This is not the time for rugged individualism or independence. Join forces where you can. And do not resist the momentum or trends about you. Instead, use them to your advantage.

Your Next Step: You will receive favorable attention and help where you give it. This is a time to forge new alliances and strengthen old ones. Recognize the cycles of mood and movement about you and cooperate with them.

THE CHANGING LINES

6: You may have been sabotaged by motives and behavior which are opposed to your best interests. If this sabotage has occurred within you, fix it.

5: Deeper attitudes and values may be shifting, causing irritation or hesitation. Embrace the change and what it leads you toward.

4: You are in danger of overreacting or becoming impetuous. Take care to preserve a sensible perspective and simple style.

3: Emotional control is important. Moderation in attitude can help you preserve your dignity and protect your welfare.

2: The situation is unstable and intense reactions are possible. Temperance is essential.

1: Resolve confusion and ambiguity by clarifying your purpose, role, and goals, then stay on target.

Unchanging: Seek out where you are too isolated from others or your higher self. Try to resolve disparities in your beliefs, plans, goals, and methods. Do this for elements within yourself as well as between you and others. Work to dissolve dichotomies and antagonism. Progress here will release new creative energy for collaboration.

31. Shared Benefits

All of life is based on cooperation at the most basic levels. We depend on the support of others to assist in providing for our most basic needs. Our careers depend on a market for our services or products. Our personal happiness depends on the friendship and assistance of others. Your current situation is one which highlights this principle of shared benefits. If these benefits are not obvious to you, then examine the object of your inquiry and its problems and possibilities. Your goal should be to build trust and rapport. This will provide the focus for enabling you to promote a relationship of shared benefits.

Your Resistance: Be careful about trying to impose your concept of what you believe would be helpful. This is no time for highly individualistic thinking or competitiveness. Reject defensive and combative styles of operation.

Your Next Step: Study the situation or persons as if they were a dear friend whom you want to help. Know their issues, needs, problems as well as what is enjoyable and fulfilling to them. Only then can you be sure your efforts will not be intrusive or harmful.

THE CHANGING LINES

6: So far, your thinking is too abstract and theoretical. This situation calls for pragmatic action.

5: Self-serving interests and motives will produce insignificant results. Expand the breadth of your outlook and goals.

4: You can attract the trust and cooperation you need by demonstrating to others your integrity and innate goodwill.

3: Trying to impress others by flaunting your strengths or needs will be seen as manipulative. Develop a more mature approach and stick to it.

2: Take a break until you know more about this situation. Some of your assumptions are naive and may humiliate you if acted upon.

1: Early hints and warnings are alerting you to significant potential for good or bad. Just observe matters for the moment.

Unchanging: Before you can share in the good potential of this situation, you must be more open and trusting. Don't think in terms of "What is in it for me," but rather in terms of "What is in it for us." This attitude will direct your awareness and behavior to the correct path.

In the end, the elements which stand the test of time are those we must treasure the most. These are the enduring values and traditions which have proven their merit and helpfulness to us. They are the principles which provide clarity to our thinking and stability to our activities. Like old friends, we must now turn to them for guidance and support for this situation. If innovation or creative action must be taken, begin by a fresh interpretation or adaptation of some familiar principle or tradition. Continue to honor your most cherished values, but, if necessary, apply them in new, skillful ways.

Your Resistance: Avoid both extremes of stubborn adherence to old habits and the rapid acceptance of the latest fad. Beware superficial or temporary solutions. Begin your analysis by a thoughtful return to your fundamental values.

Your Next Step: Ponder on the original purpose that has led to your involvement in this situation. Be aware of your deepest principles and long term goals. This will provide the proper framework for correct plans and activities leading to the right approach to this situation.

THE CHANGING LINES

6: Speculate less and focus on the good you can accomplish. Your tendencies to worry and fuss are only adding to your problems.

5: Your style of analyzing this situation is either too sublime and abstract or too mechanical and simplistic. Get real.

4: Pragmatism is lacking. You need to reappraise your objectives and what you believe can be achieved.

3: Your response has been based on your reactions and is too superficial. Begin again from a more inward and principled basis.

2: Seek a calm and moderate focus for your thoughts and behavior. This will prevent distractions into incorrect paths.

1: Impatience is your greatest risk. Don't try to accomplish so much so quickly. With your help, the situation will evolve at its pace.

Unchanging: Seek inspiration from your higher self. Consult your most cherished values and then make plans for activities that honor them. Impulsive or reactive behavior at this time will distract you and may lead to misfortune.

33. Stepping Back

You are flying headlong into conflict. If you continue to proceed in this direction, you will trap yourself in a frustrating, exhausting dilemma that could easily be avoided. What you need to do is to take a step or two back and reevaluate the assumptions and reasons that led you to pursue this direction. The conflict may be external, involving work or loved ones; it may also be internal, a conflict between your values and your desires. At present, you are too close to these issues to realize that you have erred; only when you detach from the pressures you have imposed on yourself will it become possible to clarify the best way to proceed. Try to look at this situation from the perspective of your higher self—from the perspective of the greatest measure of wisdom, goodwill, and cooperation you possess.

Your Resistance: You are over-emphasizing unimportant, and perhaps even imaginary, failures, insults, disappointments, or hurts. You need to discover that you can lift your attention above these things and achieve a healthier perspective.

Your Next Step: You must clean up your inner landscape before you can resolve the outer elements of this issue. This may require forgiving others, dropping long-held resentments, or reactivating your self-esteem. Learn to call on the wisdom and goodwill of the higher self to help you take these steps.

THE CHANGING LINES

6: Stop clinging to conditions that have faded in importance. Pour your energies into the problems of today, not yesterday.

5: The best way to step back is to step up—by identifying with the direction and purpose of the higher self. It holds the key for breaking the logjam.

4: You are prolonging a stagnant condition by stubbornly refusing to look at reality. Broaden your understanding; loosen up.

3: You are caught in a long sequence of consequences resulting from your own selfish behavior in the past. The only way to break the cycle is to heal or redeem your selfishness.

2: Your only enemy is your own indifference; you need to renew your interest in what you are doing.

1: You have waited too long to act; now you are trapped in a net of your own making. Do not try to fight your way out; accept these restrictions graciously and wait for a better time.

Unchanging: You are heading in directions that are not in accord with the plan of the higher self. Remove yourself from these situations as quickly as you can, and renew your ties with the wisdom within you.

You have achieved a measure of control and power in some area of your life. If you have the imagination to envision it, it is now possible to expand the sphere of your authority and influence. To seize the opportunity of growth being presented, however, it will be necessary to approach this step forward with humility, respect for others, and patience. New authority and power can destroy as well as create; it is therefore of great importance to approach this time of expanding influence as a duty to perform, rather than a reward. At the level of your personality, it will be necessary to expand your tolerance of others, your capacity to endure, and the intelligence to act wisely—as well as your sense of commitment to inner purpose. In your communion with the higher self, it will be necessary to learn to rely more forthrightly on the wisdom and will of divine guidance.

Your Resistance: Any trace of self-centeredness at this time will cancel out the real promise of this expanding influence. Selfishness shrinks the sphere of your influence; to be in step with expansiveness, you must act with goodwill and inclusiveness.

Your Next Step: The real source of this power lies in your ability to tap the purpose being served—the will of a people being governed, the direction of a business, or the plan of your higher self. Try to act as an intelligent and loving agent of this inner purpose.

THE CHANGING LINES

6: You have over-estimated the depth of your personal authority; you are being used by others as a puppet for their own convenience.

5: You may be tempted to reject the guidance of the higher self. Be sure assumptions of the personality do not obscure legitimate guidance.

4: Be sure the values that guide you are wholesome—and in harmony with the overall purpose you are striving to serve.

3: The focus of your expanding authority is behind the scenes, in a supportive role. Do not get caught in the limelight.

2: You are making a spectacle by rebelling against genuine authority. Become a constructive participant!

1: Be sure you are honoring the intent of your own ideals and highest motivations before exercising power.

Unchanging: Your enthusiasm does not match your ideas or your plans. If you do not want your whole effort to fall apart, it will be necessary to think through exactly what you propose to do with this expanded influence.

35. Enlightenment

Whatever the object of your inquiry, the insight you need in order to understand it is within your reach. To tap it, you need to focus your need to know, your ability to respond, and your love of truth so that they create an invocation that will bring this wisdom into your conscious understanding. In many cases, this insight will come as an intuition of the higher self, but it may well come from other sources as well. A friend or acquaintance may provide an object lesson that awakens you to a new level of understanding—or a book or TV show may set in motion a line of thought that ends in new comprehension. It may even just well up from unconscious sources into your conscious mind when the time is right. In any event, this new wisdom will only transform your life if you recognize it, think about it, comprehend it, and then integrate it into your existing values, beliefs, and behavior.

Your Resistance: An untrained mind, a mind that habitually looks for all its answers in the physical plane, or a mind that thinks it knows it all, will have a very difficult time responding to enlightenment. It will have to be trained in basic thinking skills first.

Your Next Step: Good ideas are meaningless unless they are given appropriate expression in life. Once you are enlightened, be sure to follow through by integrating your new inspiration into daily living.

THE CHANGING LINES

6: Do not overreact to the new wisdom that enlightens you. Take time to digest these new insights, so that when you do act, it will be appropriately.

5: You should apply your new insights to nurturing the growth of people you care for. In this way, it will open up new avenues of growth for you.

4: Protect your ideas from others, lest they ridicule you for them—or distort them to the point where you are plunged back into confusion.

3: Share your ideas with others. They may be able to enrich them in ways you have not considered.

2: You may be substituting optimism for clear insight. It is not enough to feel good about plans; they must be practical as well.

1: Others are trying to persuade you, or perhaps coerce you, into thinking the same way they do. You are in danger of aligning with harmful ideas or principles. Think for yourself!

Unchanging: Your mind is working on a higher wavelength than ever before. Much progress can be made if you can learn to respond consistently to this wavelength. Make this a high priority in your efforts to grow.

36. Sabotage

You are being forced to deal with movements, ideas, or people who have no interest in your well-being and are, in fact, determined to sabotage your efforts to grow. This does not mean that you or your plans will be defeated, however. It just means that you must find a way to continue pursuing your growth and plans in alternate ways. In most cases, this sabotage will not print out as overt acts of opposition. It will be more subtle—the undermining of your self-esteem, the criticizing of your modus operandi, or even just the planting of tiny seeds of doubt that will grow and spread. It may even come from friends or loved ones who do not want to see you change. It is therefore important to examine carefully the full range of people, groups, traditions, and ideas that you rely on for guidance, suggestions, and support. Is this support truly helping you to grow and prosper—or is it in fact sabotaging your best efforts?

Your Resistance: The strongest force of sabotage may be within yourself. Old habits may try to sabotage new ones. Old biases will war against new understanding. A poor self-esteem may prevent forward progress. Stop shooting yourself in the foot.

Your Next Step: The more you learn to nurture your work, growth, or service with peace and love, the more you will build an immunity to sabotage. Let the higher self nourish your awareness daily.

THE CHANGING LINES

6: The forces of sabotage are waning. If you will be patient, you can outlast them, and reestablish a forward pattern of growth and progress.

5: If you examine this situation from a higher perspective, you may find that the apparent forces of sabotage are actually working toward your eventual success. Adjust your behavior accordingly.

4: Conditions are heading toward collapse. It is probably too late to prevent it, so take steps to minimize its impact on you.

3: You are about to discover a hidden source of sabotage. Think before you react; do not poison opportunity as well as opposition.

2: Learn to deal with sabotage with an even hand. If you react to threat by becoming paranoid, you will be sabotaging yourself. Do not overdo it.

1: You are inviting sabotage by advertising your ideas and plans too openly. Keep a low profile; don't dare competitors, friends, or colleagues to outdo you, lest they do.

Unchanging: The limitations you are enduring are designed to help you learn to rely on the strengths and qualities of the higher self, rather than the expertise of the personality.

37. Heritage

In the solar system, the planets revolve about the sun. Each of us similarly revolves around some central core that is the source of our thinking, acting, and identity. For many of us, this central core is our physical family. Indeed, the Chinese name for this hexagram is "family." For some people, however, the concept of "family" needs to be expanded; for a nun or priest, for instance, the church would be their family. In this sense, our family becomes whatever we identify with most closely; the central source from which we draw our strength, resolve, and sense of purpose. When this hexagram arises, it suggests that our personal growth is transpiring within a family context—either our flesh and blood family or our spiritual family. We need to pay more attention to the role we are playing within the family, and make sure that our private goals are still consistent and in harmony with the larger ones of our heritage.

Your Resistance: Most of the ties that bind the flesh and blood family are physical and emotional. Take care not to let these ties blind you to the mental and spiritual realities of life, which should be the true source of identity and nurturing love.

Your Next Step: It is a great achievement to learn that your true heritage lies in your divine birthright, rather than in your ancestral lineage, your ethnic legacy, or your cultural background.

THE CHANGING LINES

6: Your true heritage lies at the level of the soul. Learn to build your sense of identity and strength on this connection.

5: You are not embodying the full potential of your heritage as completely as you might. Strive for a greater expression of your spiritual legacy.

4: Learn to rely on the stability that comes from a solid sense of heritage.

3: You are coming dangerously close to damaging relationships that could benefit you greatly later in life. It's time to start mending fences.

2: Attempts to assert your individuality will draw counter efforts to keep you in line. Little can be gained by open rebellion.

1: You may be overemphasizing the importance of your genetic heritage, forgetting that each of us is first and foremost a member of the family of humanity.

Unchanging: You are too submerged in traditional roles and obligations. As a result, you have stopped thinking for yourself; when others say "jump," you jump. This is creating a deep level of dissatisfaction within you. Get expert help in resolving this conflict.

38. Ambiguity

Your efforts to grow have led you into a state of confusion, frustration, and uncertainty. There do not seem to be any clear cut answers to your questions. If they regard moral issues, there are always special cases which seem to undermine the moral platitudes you have been taught. If they regard ethics, you keep running into situations where your ethical principles seem to backfire. As impossible as it may seem to escape from this morass of ambiguity, however, be assured that it can be done. You can train the mind to examine the confusing elements and contradictions of daily life, comparing them with the solid principles of the higher self. You can also train the mind to recognize and eliminate areas of contradiction within your own thinking.

Your Resistance: As long as you prefer to think in terms of black and white, right and wrong, you will be prey to ambiguity. As long as you think a discussion ought to be a debate, rather than an exploration of ideas, you will succumb to confusion. You must learn to pursue truth for its own sake.

Your Next Step: Try to look at the confusing issues of life from the goodwill, wisdom, and joy of the higher self. If you do not know how to proceed in learning this, seek out the help of those who can teach or guide you.

THE CHANGING LINES

6: You have let yourself become defensive, but this only heightens the misunderstanding. You will have to embrace the whole picture before you can correct all the misunderstandings.

5: Your confusion or uncertainty is the result of an inaccurate impression you have formed about another person. Correct it before you deepen the mess.

4: There is a basic conflict between your expectations and your values. You need to establish a more coherent sense of priority.

3: Try to see the good or helpful elements in what is happening to you. Your belief that current events are harmful or threatening is making it impossible to interact rationally with them.

2: You are being drawn away from previously held beliefs and prejudices. If you fight this shift, you will suffer greatly; if you cooperate, by opening your mind to new possibilities, you will benefit greatly.

1: You are missing the obvious. Do not act until you have gained a clearer understanding. It may be helpful to ask a friend or counselor to assist you.

Unchanging: You are in danger of becoming polarized by a heated issue. This is unwise. Remain as flexible, tolerant, and forgiving as possible.

39. Hurdles

Your growth and prosperity appear to be blocked by circumstances, restrictions, or obstacles. You may feel that you are in a "dead end" job—or trapped in some situation. Before you can escape this "trap," however, you are going to have to learn two things. First, the circumstances that seem to trap and limit you are actually hurdles you are meant to learn to overcome. Second, by and large, the real problem is not the outer circumstance but the inner hurdles which keep you from dealing effectively with the outer ones. In other words, it is not the job that limits people—but their attitudes toward their work. Learn to put joy into your work and you will discover you can enjoy it. Basically, in whatever circumstances you find yourself at present, it is important to assume that they represent your best opportunity to grow. Stop resenting them and rebelling against them— "kicking against the pricks," as Paul put it. Accept them for what they are and reap the benefit of learning to leap over these hurdles.

Your Resistance: Your "suffering" is largely self-imposed. You likewise hold the key to ending it, and can do so at any time, just by accepting the limits of your life maturely and striving to do the best you can with what you've got.

Your Next Step: Accept these hurdles gracefully, then apply your full effort to taking them in stride.

THE CHANGING LINES

6: The breakthrough you are looking for can come by consulting someone who is wiser than you.

5: The real hurdle you need to leap over is the gap you have created between the personality and your higher self. Let the wisdom within you guide you and show you the correct way to proceed.

4: Stubbornness and pride are preventing you from seeing the opportunities within apparent obstacles.

3: You are exhausting yourself by jousting with the phantom soldiers of external circumstances. You need to refocus on your true values.

2: The "hurdles" you face are a printout of commitments you freely made in the past. Do not try to push them aside.

1: The hurdle before you cannot be removed for the near future. Do not let it become any larger by reacting angrily or resentfully toward it. Accept it as an important part of your life—and strive to use it to your advantage.

Unchanging: You are being your own worst enemy. Until you learn to love yourself and accept yourself as a mature adult, you will continue to trip over your own lack of self-esteem and uncertainty.

40. Recreation

The best way to handle the crises and challenges of the present moment is to loosen up a bit and relax. No matter how serious the problems of the day may be, it will do you no good to wear yourself down by constantly struggling with and worrying about them. You need to detach from these pressures and unwind a little. Clear your mind and let it enjoy life a bit. Then, when life forces you to deal with the pressures of the day again, you will be able to approach them with a fresh perspective and a renewed sense of hope. Just be sure that the mode of recreation you choose is truly relaxing and renewing. Select an activity that allows you to "re-create" your vitality, your plans, and even your modes of acting.

Your Resistance: You are stuck in established patterns of behavior. Loosen up. Don't take this issue quite as seriously as you have been. Be willing to yield to the suggestions and insights of others.

Your Next Step: Conditions in your life are trying to help you break free from something that has long enslaved you. The more you cling to these limiting conditions, the more frustrated you will get. It is therefore important to detach yourself from whatever it is that is suppressing your growth.

THE CHANGING LINES

6: Events are propelling you toward a turning point or time of resolution. Do not fight the tide. If you keep your wits about you, the journey may well end in triumph.

5: You have pushed yourself to the point where you are beginning to succumb to weaknesses and temptations which normally do not affect you. You need to recollect yourself and turn your focus once again on the inner strength that nourishes and guides you.

4: You have let others cling to you in unhealthy ways. You will know little rest until you find the courage to disengage from these people.

3: Others may try to dissuade you from your plans. Do not heed them—they are just envious. Your plans are in harmony with the need of the moment.

2: There are those who are trying to discredit you. Do not fall into their trap by responding openly to their innuendos. If you preserve your dignity and hold to your values, you will emerge even stronger than before.

1: You have been forced into a period of inactivity. Use it wisely, to prepare for coming opportunity.

Unchanging: An internal release is helping you let go of old attitudes or habits that have crippled you.

41. Loss

Two of the most basic energies of life are gain and loss. In the I Ching, loss comes first, as hexagram 41. Gain follows in the next breath, as hexagram 42. To understand these two phenomena, they must be seen as the two halves of the same activity. In fact, much of what we label "loss" actually turns out to be "gain," when we see the situation more clearly. Just so, much of the gain we yearn for often represents a step back, once we comprehend the full implications of what we have been striving toward. At this stage in your growth, you are probably more aware of losses and sliding backwards than you are of gains and accomplishments. No matter how hard you try, you seem to lose ground. You need to understand that you are not actually going in reverse. It is an illusion created by your own limited perspective. Focus instead on your values, skills, and insights. Are these growing and expanding, in spite of the superficial appearance of loss?

Your Resistance: You have managed to convince yourself that you are losing ground, even though you are not. The sense of "loss" is an imaginary one, generated by an inner sense of loss or inadequacy.

Your Next Step: Stop magnifying the aspects of life that seem to be going wrong for you, and start working to build on the foundation of that which is healthy, stable, and productive in your life.

THE CHANGING LINES

6: The best way to help others at this time is by setting an example of what it means to endure loss or setback gracefully.

5: Your old sources of motivation are wearing down. It is time to establish new, healthier goals based on your future, not your past.

4: You need to lose some "weight" psychologically, especially the excess weight of self-importance and self-centeredness. Stop blaming others—and life.

3: Do not try to judge present events with worn out standards. The meaning of what is happening to you is very much different than you suspect. Update!

2: You have been daring life to knock that chip off your shoulder for quite some time now, and it finally has. You have no one to blame but yourself for the seeming severity of your losses.

1: The setbacks you are suffering are no reflection on you or your efforts. Take them in stride, acting with common sense and prudence.

Unchanging: You are in danger of becoming a chronic bellyacher. Learn to celebrate the good things in life before you become hopelessly estranged from your own inner life.

42. Gain

This is one of those rare times when growth comes easily and rapidly. It is therefore important not to take it for granted, or assume it will always be this easy—or this rewarding. Do not make assumptions that overrate your talent, skill, or ability, just because everything is coming together for you at the moment. Once this moment has passed, will you have integrated the new skills and abilities you are learning? Will you be able to act so skillfully and creatively in far more difficult—or even dangerous—circumstances? The gain of the moment is substantial, but is it something that can be preserved in less auspicious times? This is the real question that needs to be answered.

Your Resistance: Even though you may not be aware of it, your resistance is most likely at an all time high during any period of rapid gain. Gains bring new responsibilities, opportunities, and commitments, all of which charge up the force of resistance within ourself. Beware of lethargy, moral ambivalence, and worry at this time—they are the signs your resistance is hard at work, sabotaging your gains.

Your Next Step: Make sure that the gains of this time serve to produce stronger values and a clearer sense of direction. Once you define what these are, then evaluate how you can reinvest your gains of the present for further gains in the future.

THE CHANGING LINES

6: The forces of gain are beginning to wane. While you may still feel invincible, you are in fact on the very edge of falling from your high status. Exercise great care.

5: Generosity is the ultimate achievement of gain.

4: You are part of a larger group which is reaping the rewards of gain. Your best opportunity for growth, therefore, lies in trying to serve the group as a whole more effectively.

3: Do not make assumptions about your talents and your future which would be shattered by any results less than what you are enjoying now.

2: You are riding high tide. Be careful not to become cocky or overly confident—accept your good fortune with humility and gratitude.

1: This is a good time to expand your responsibilities or duties; you can handle it. Strive to be more productive in what you do.

Unchanging: The forces of gain are definitely at work, but behind the scenes. To harness them, you must invoke them—but first, you must know where to find them. The true answer lies within.

43. Firm Resolve

Many people think that their lives are guided by out-side forces—karma, kismet, fate, or luck. What they are overlooking is that the strongest force in our lives is our own motivation—our will to grow, our will to serve, or our will to triumph over obstacles. The key to generating this motivation is to understand that it should be our personal expression of a universal motivation—for example, the divine impulse to grow or the divine impulse to love. As we mature, we hammer this abstract, divine force into a firm, un-wavering force of individual resolve. This firm resolve not only gives us the power to act, but also serves to shape the larger fabric of events and activi-ties which becomes the tapestry of our life.

Your Resistance: You are too easily manipulated and controlled by others to develop a firm resolve of your own—especially a motivation empowered by inner forces. You must learn to be guided by your values and ideals, rather than your wishes and the popular opinions of the masses.

Your Next Step: You are going to have to take a stand in some major aspect of your life, and then follow through on it, regardless of the consequences. Do not try to set others up for the blame in case it backfires; face the issue squarely and express your principles as clearly as you can. Have the courage of your con-victions.

THE CHANGING LINES

6: The opportunity to serve is unparalleled. If your motive is an altruistic one, you can accomplish much.

5: You are facing great odds—far more than one person can manage. But do not despair; you can find help and support if you seek out others with a similar resolve.

4: You are confusing firm resolve for stubbornness. As a result, you have drawn to yourself a series of problems which impede your progress.

3: As long as you do not lose your nerve, you have the upper hand in the struggle that is occurring. Hold fast to what you know is right.

2: Rash actions are not a good substitute for a firm resolve. Resolution implies that your actions are supported by careful, deliberate thinking.

1: Since you lack the resolve to do much on your own, you must identify with groups or movements that will carry you along with them. Choose wisely.

Unchanging: You are discovering that not all of your acts and goals match your values and ideals. In fact, many of them conflict seriously with one another, thereby creating uncertainty and instability. You need to reconcile these differences before you harm yourself irreparably.

44. Hypocrisy

You are caught in a web of your own weaving. Perhaps you have gone on record supporting one course of action, only to realize that it is no longer convenient to pursue that program. Or you may have found that current events expose the folly of earlier beliefs you embraced militantly. Three things can happen. You can repudiate your earlier convictions and embrace new ones which suit the need of the moment. You can stonewall it, allowing the present situation to degerate into hostility and unhappiness. Or, you can undergo a major transformation of character, in which you reconcile your values and convictions with the needs and rights of others, society, and yourself. Either one of the first two options would just be a quick fix, of course, and rightfully expose you to charges of hypocrisy. In pursuing the third option, by contrast, you confront the actual conflict within your character—the conflict that has arisen from unintegrated values, goals, ideals, and beliefs—and make the effort to eliminate the hypocrisy.

Your Resistance: No one likes to think of themselves as a hypocrite. But the refusal to examine and revise your values, ideals, and beliefs as necessary can lead to great inner turmoil and confusion.

Your Next Step: Growth can only occur by reordering your priorities and behavior, so that they express your deepest beliefs and humanitarian concerns.

THE CHANGING LINES

6: Others may ridicule the ideals and authority that you represent or hold dear. Do not respond. They cannot hurt you unless you let them "get to you."

5: You can depend upon your values and convictions to give you strength in a difficult situation. Just make sure you are not short-circuiting them in some foolish way.

4: You may be right in your criticism of others, but you are setting a demoralizing tone by being harshly critical or suspicious. Always remember that the first rule of ethics is to treat others as you would like to be treated yourself.

3: You are tempted to overreact to a situation that does not deserve so much attention. Is this really an issue you want to make a stand on?

2: Stop blaming others for what is essentially your own problem. Clean up your share of the mess before scolding others.

1: Do not get caught up in a holy war against the hypocrisy in others. Inspect your own mental household, to make sure everything is in order.

Unchanging: You are called on to set a high and noble example for your group—or even society. Set aside personal issues and rise to the challenge.

45. Planning

Strong forces are coming together. They will be released in the "overnight success" of Hexagram #46, but first they must be gathered, assembled, and staged. This is a stage in development that we commonly call preparation or planning. It is important to approach this stage with great patience, lest we try to act prematurely, before all of the forces are in place. It is also important to approach this phase wisely. Through the right use of intelligent planning, we can do a lot to shape the way in which opportunities, opposition, and support will unfold. This is therefore a time to quietly but vigorously line up allies, clear away potential obstacles, rehearse the ideal course to pursue, acquire necessary skills, and do whatever else is required to lay a proper foundation for your success.

Your Resistance: You cannot harness the forces of success by being passive and "going with the flow." Life is giving you an opportunity to take some initiative and shape the outcome of this phase of your life and work. If you fail to seize this initiative now, you will not be in control later.

Your Next Step: Take the time to review what you hope will happen regarding your inquiry. Develop a plan that would lead to your goal. What do you need to do to implement this plan?

THE CHANGING LINES

6: The plans you are developing and implementing will become the structure for future efforts. Build wisely!

5: By aligning with the plans of your own higher self, you tap the authority and power to develop and implement successful plans in your daily life.

4: You sense the goal but not the timing, nor the preliminary steps involved. Step back and review these issues before you create mischief.

3: Beware of envy within yourself, lest it encourage you to intrude where you have no right to be.

2: You are in a perfect position to help someone else. Do not become so absorbed in your own plans that you tune out the needs of others.

1: Like so many people, you are essentially stumbling through life as if in a fog. You need to define some central goals and create a pathway toward progress.

Unchanging: The ideal plan is already established and known to you at unconscious levels. Try to act in harmony with this ideal plan. You will become aware of it as it begins to manifest.

You are enjoying a period of sudden breakthrough or "overnight success." Keep in mind, however, that most such successes are nothing more than overnight recognition of years and years of effort, careful planning, and struggle. To understand fully what is happening to you, therefore, it is important to see the antecedents leading up to this time of advancement and sudden progress. Nothing is happening miraculously or magically; it is all the inevitable consequence of intelligent activity. For this reason, it is equally important not to take this level of success for granted; you must continue to nurture your work and efforts in order to prolong the momentum you are now enjoying. Nowhere is this more clear than in issues of personal and spiritual growth. The visible signs of growth may come in short, quick bursts in which you make quantum leaps forward; but the actual work of growth requires a commitment to slow but steady, consistent effort to change and improve.

Your Resistance: There is a tendency to be satisfied with small steps and small achievements. Do not rest on the laurels you are now receiving. You are like a plant that has popped through the soil in spring— your growth is only now beginning!

Your Next Step: You need to continue on with the same program or plan that brought you to this point. In other words, your next step should be the same as your last step!

THE CHANGING LINES

6: The success that has brought you to this point did not represent true growth for you. You now stand at the beginning of a new cycle of genuine growth.

5: A sudden glitch in the smooth unfoldment of your plans does not foretell disaster; address the problem, fix it, and be on your way again.

4: People who ignored you before will be reappearing, offering to help. Do not scorn them, but find ways to incorporate them into your efforts.

3: You are in harmony with higher inspiration. Let it guide you in your efforts to grow.

2: There is a difference between wishing for growth or success and actually achieving it. It is time to stop dreaming and start doing.

1: You are trying to do too much too quickly. Take on a project or goal that you can handle.

Unchanging: The real breakthrough that has occurred is hidden behind events that most people do not understand. You may be the only one who can appreciate the growth that has unfolded.

47. Reactiveness

You have become your own worst enemy, impeding your growth and progress by unjustified reactions to your problems. As a result, you have become trapped in reactive patterns of worry, fear, escapism, and accusations. In relationships, for instance, you tend to blame others for the problems you deal with—instead of examining the ways you have contributed to misunderstandings, behaved immaturely, and criticized harshly. As a result, you have become an "unhappy camper"—and it is no one's fault but your own. This also means that no one but yourself can reverse this pattern. To do so, you must stop seeing life as the enemy. Learn to like your work, instead of resenting it, by enriching it with your own cheerfulness. Learn to like others, instead of constantly degrading them, by dwelling on the good qualities they have. Stop letting events control you irrationally. There is no law forcing you to be angry, impatient, and irritable, after all. You have the option of being a kind-hearted, helpful, and considerate person.

Your Resistance: You feel justified, perhaps even righteous, is believing that others are the cause of your misery. You are kidding yourself.

Your Next Step: Unless you begin treating life and others more rationally, you will soon be on a downward spiral of reactiveness which may be impossible to stop.

THE CHANGING LINES

6: You need to regain control of the situation you are asking about; seek to act from the highest level of maturity and wisdom you can reach.

5: Replace the reactiveness of your emotions with a consistent responsiveness to the ideals and purpose of the higher self.

4: You are not only trapped in the present, but also in the past. Try forgiving people who have hurt you and understanding situations that seem senseless.

3: Instead of succumbing to your emotional reactiveness, try responding to the potential goodness within others, within events, and within circumstance.

2: Do not assume that everyone who says he or she can help you will be able to. Make sure they will be a constructive influence, not a harmful one.

1: You are searching for answers to your problems, but you are looking in all the wrong places. As long as you long for a quick, easy fix to your problems, you will be unable to make much progress.

Unchanging: You have tortured yourself to the point of exhaustion. You desperately need to consult expert help to assist you in recreating a healthier attitude toward yourself, others, and life.

48. Inner Oneness

At this stage in your development, growth must be nurtured from the inner well of oneness—the point of spiritual purpose within you. You may be very much involved in physical life—engaged in business, raising a family, or serving the community—yet you need to see your real growth not in terms of physical achievements but in terms of refining your spiritual self-expression. This level of growth will be most readily observed in your thoughts and motives. They will become steadily less selfish and self-centered as you identify with the purposes and plans that unite you with the rest of humanity—and all of life. The focus of your priorities and motives will gradually shift from the highly personal "me" of the personality to the spiritual perspectives of the higher self.

Your Resistance: There is a difference between identifying with the masses and identifying with the spiritual purpose within humanity. Too much responsiveness to the cries and clamors of the masses can blind the otherwise clear sight of a wise person.

Your Next Step: Learn to identify with the true source of wisdom and destiny governing your work, your primary relationships, and your interests.

THE CHANGING LINES

6: It is not enough to know. You must also serve.

5: You can master the lesson before you only if you understand and practice correct sacrifice.

4: By attuning frequently to the inner oneness, you will find your mind is becoming reoriented to spiritual priorities.

3: You can act most effectively if you choose to act behind the scenes, out of the limelight.

2: You are too deeply engrossed in this situation to see clearly. You need a sabbatical or time off to recharge your batteries and review your assumptions.

1: You are far too shallow and superficial in your dealings with others and life. Strive to infuse your acts and attitudes with joy and enthusiasm.

Unchanging: Whether you recognize it or not, you are part of a much larger group of individuals, both incarnate and discarnate. If you become aware of this group, you can call upon it for guidance and support.

49. Adjustment

You are beginning to question assumptions and beliefs that made sense to you before. This period of questioning and perhaps even doubting may be disturbing and unsettling to you, but it represents a healthy stage in your growth. You are finally beginning to use the light of the mind to examine life and its meaning. As you discover ideas and beliefs that have become dead ends for you, of course, you will need to discard them and replace them with new convictions and guiding ideals. In this way, you will make the adjustments in your thoughts, habits, values, and priorities that will allow you to continue growing. Unless these inner adjustments are made, you will end up stagnating.

Your Resistance: Many of your most cherished beliefs and assumptions will be challenged during the time of adjustment. If you cling to these beliefs, unwilling to let go, you can cause great damage to your inner psychology. Accept the need for adjustment gracefully.

Your Next Step: The higher self is calling you to discover the source of joy and beauty within yourself. Contentment in this life cannot be achieved by lusting after material wealth or goods; it must be cultivated as a dynamic inner presence. Discovering this inner presence of contentment is a major part of the work of adjustment.

THE CHANGING LINES

6: As the required changes are made, fresh light pours into your mind. Celebrate the addition of new energy in your life.

5: Let your own intuition guide you in determining what changes to make and how to make them.

4: You are confusing escapism with constructive change. Avoiding problems and confrontations is never a recipe for growth.

3: You have changed more than you give yourself credit for. Update yourself and start using the potential you have tapped.

2: Do not try to achieve change by making dramatic, irreversible adjustments in your outer life. The adjustments you need to make are all within yourself—in attitudes, habits, beliefs, and convictions.

1: You have let others talk you into embracing ideas and values which are not helpful to you. Return to the heritage of your younger days for guidance.

Unchanging: You are being called on to discover a transcendent presence in your life, and then adjust priorities, duties, and goals to embody this higher presence. Remember: "The many are called, the few are chosen."

Many issues that have confused or distracted you will suddenly become clear. You may not as yet know what to do with this new insight, but it will at least help you understand some of the struggles of the past. Just make sure you strive to interpret these revelations from the wisest and noblest perspective within yourself. After all, revelation can be a two-edged sword. It can inspire you with the splendor and truth of divine order—or it can strip bare the imperfections of your own thinking, the acts of others, or the efforts of society. In working with the opportunity of revelation, therefore, we must learn to be like Mary when the angels revealed to her the role she would play in the coming of the Christ. She was unsure of what it all meant, but held the revelation in her heart, where she pondered on it. It is important at times of revelation to avoid getting bogged down in an analysis of details; grasp the larger picture that is emerging and hold it in your heart, pondering it.

Your Resistance: Many people erect elaborate defense mechanisms so that they can avoid facing the truth about themselves. If you are one of them, the time of revelation may seem to deal more with tearing down these barriers than anything else.

Your Next Step: A revelation will only become active in your life if you integrate it into your daily lifestyle. Live the truth as it has been revealed to you.

THE CHANGING LINES

6: The opportunity exists to tap a rich measure of joy and incorporate it into your attitudes and lifestyle.

5: The growth you are trying to inspire in others must be paralleled by similar growth in your own character, wisdom, and creative skills. Strive for the highest—it is within your reach!

4: If you continue to hold on to regrets and guilt concerning the past, you will miss the fulfillment which can be yours in the present.

3: Do not belittle the role you play. It has meaning within the larger scheme of things, even though you are probably unable to grasp why or how.

2: You are confusing rebellion for revelation. You need to adopt a whole new course of action, founded on more substantial values and principles.

1: Your understanding of the situation at hand is distorted by your own feelings. You need to seek out a more objective, complete perspective.

Unchanging: You are trapped within cultural traditions and prejudices that prevent you from fully grasping the revelation that you, and those linked to you, need in order to take the next step. Pray for guidance in penetrating these barriers, even though others will make it their business to stop you.

51. Explosiveness

Explosive forces have been allowed to build up, and they are about to be released, stirring up the outer events and conditions of your life. While no one likes to have the basic quietness of life disturbed, these explosions will not necessarily be harmful ones. They are, in fact, part of your larger pattern of personal growth, in that they will lead you to new opportunities, new realizations, or perhaps even greater accomplishments. It is therefore paramount to meet these explosive conditions with equanamity and poise. If you respond with explosiveness of your own—fear, anger, or bitterness—you will expose yourself to serious psychological damage. On the other hand, if you respond with reverence for God and a steady aspiration to make the most of these times, you will be prepared to seize opportunities as they present themselves.

Your Resistance: Explosive circumstances often represent times when you are able to see that your goals are out of harmony with those of the higher self—or life itself. Use this time to redefine goals and methods so that they are in line with higher intent.

Your Next Step: Do not leave anything to chance. Take control of any aspects of life you may have been ignoring; strive to regain control of circumstances that have blown up in your face. A more refined, enlightened measure of self-control is required.

THE CHANGING LINES

6: Even though you seem to be powerless to act, you can gain great authority by acting with self-restraint and inner guidance. Set a noble example.

5: The forcefulness with which you have acted has complicated matters. You will need to take a new tact if you hope to become a healing force.

4: You are making a mountain out of a molehill, thereby blinding yourself (and others) to the real issues involved.

3: A seemingly random event will explode in your face. It is not random at all, however, but a message from your higher self to make needed changes before it is too late.

2: You have created the forces of explosiveness that threaten you, through your volatile reactions to the ordinary conditions of life. Calm down.

1: You have allowed your interest in growing to stagnate in too many ways. You need an explosion or two to reawaken yourself.

Unchanging: It is important to make sure that all of the pent-up pressures leading to this condition of explosiveness are discharged. Clear the air completely before trying to initiate compromise or change.

52. Inner Pulling

In contrast with the explosive nature of Hexagram 51, the forces of this time tend to pull your attention inward, toward the center of your being. As a result, you may experience a certain measure of dissatisfaction with the superficiality of daily life, wondering, "Is that all there is?" The answer, of course, is no. The inner life is rich with avenues awaiting our exploration, if we will just respond to these inner tugs and pulls and spend some time in the interior recesses of consciousness. This could be something as simple as a renewed interest in the arts or culture, leading to a more refined and creative perspective on life. Or it might result in a deliberate effort, through prayer or meditation, to cultivate an ongoing awareness of the higher self and the resources of wisdom, love, joy, and peace within us.

Your Resistance: Many people have a great fear of exploring the unknown regions of the mind and their psychology. During times of inner pulling, these people will often hide in a sudden preoccupation with the superficial details of life—like an ostrich burying its head in the sand.

Your Next Step: As the ancients advised us, "Know Thyself." The examination of our inner motives, attitudes, thoughts, and values is one of the most important studies we can undertake. Self-examination is crucial to your ongoing psychological stability.

THE CHANGING LINES

6: When you manage to light the lamp on top of the mountain, so that it shines equally on all sides, you have harnessed the full force of inner pulling.

5: You are still susceptible to the powerful influences of mass consciousness. Learn to think for yourself!

4: The practice of contacting the higher self through active meditation can lead to inner healing and new growth.

3: You are becoming poignantly aware of the conflicts which exist between your wishes and your commitments, between your desires and your values. It is time to establish a priority among these things.

2: You are trying to respond to the inner pulls and tugs, but are touching only your feelings and desires. You are enslaved by your wish life.

1: You think you have an objective perspective of all the facts, and yet you know nothing about the inner dimensions of this situation. You are blind to reality.

Unchanging: You are spending too much time dwelling in the past. Grow up! It is time to bury the past and carry what you have learned of it into the present and the future.

53. The Keynote

Growth at this time is governed by the pace or rhythm established by the inner purpose of your activity. It is important for you to attune yourself to the keynote of this rhythm and let it guide you. Do not try to push things along too quickly, lest you harm yourself and undermine your growth through excessive strain. By the same token, do not take your growth for granted and lapse into lethargy, or you will end up going nowhere fast. Take each segment of your growth as it arises and strive to learn it to its fullest, then pass on to the next. Above all, resist all temptation to take shortcuts. There may be times when the methodical repetition of certain lessons begins to seem excessive. Nonetheless, this repetition is important to the kinds of lessons you are learning. If you fail to learn complete mastery of your lessons now, you will regret your lapse later on.

Your Resistance: Impatience and restlessness are two of the great foes of true learning. Make sure you learn the lessons of this phase of your growth thoroughly. It is not just knowledge that you should be seeking, but rather mastery.

Your Next Step: Your lesson is not learned until it is fully integrated into your thoughts, attitudes, values, and behavior. In other words, you must become a living, breathing example of the lesson you are learning. Practice what you aspire to!

THE CHANGING LINES

6: You are an example that others emulate. Make sure it is the wisdom and love you express that they hunger for, and not the trappings of self-expression.
5: You are being distracted by the resistance to learning of associates and others. Neutralize it by letting yourself be guided once more by the keynote.
4: This is not a time to "learn by doing." There is no substitute for knowledge and practice.
3: Call upon lessons you have learned in the past but have forgotten to arm you with the wisdom you need to succeed now.
2: Your motive for learning is to please others. This is not healthy. Learn to respond to the impulse to grow itself.
1: Do not be afraid to make mistakes. How else do you expect to learn?

Unchanging: Do not be overwhelmed by the scope of the lessons before you. Growth is a process of transformation. It is not measured by how much information you can digest, but rather how much love and wisdom you express in applying that information. Make sure your goals for growing are in harmony with the process itself.

54. The Apprentice

Life has put you in a position where you have no choice but to learn a lesson you have otherwise managed to avoid. There is a temptation to believe that you are a victim of unfair injustice or the cruel domination of others, but this is not the case. If you are a victim at all, it is only of your refusal to learn the lessons life would teach you. The easiest course for you, therefore, is to accept the seeming imbalance in the situation as gracefully as you can, shoulder its inequities, and see what you can learn about becoming a more mature human being. Do not cry out for mercy or sympathy—the opportunity to learn a lesson you have repeatedly ignored is the divine mercy you are invoking. If you must invoke anything, make it maturity.

Your Resistance: Like a teenager opposing the authority of his or her parents, you try to gain control by rebellion. You need to understand that it is your rebelliousness that created the need for this dilemma, and the harder you rebel, the tougher you make it on yourself.

Your Next Step: Once you accept the restrictions of your circumstance gracefully, you can begin to concentrate on learning the lessons it contains. Become an apprentice in the art of living, dedicated to acquiring both maturity and mastery in every phase of human expression.

THE CHANGING LINES

6: Ultimately, we are all apprentices in the divine workshop. The ability to recognize the lessons we are learning and allow ourself to be guided by higher intelligence is the essence of inspired apprenticeship.

5: Do not blame the higher self for your own inability to seize opportunities and have faith in divine intelligence.

4: You need a major dose of humility—the recognition that life is far greater than you and cannot be fooled. Your cleverness will only trap you.

3: You have rationalized your actions so often that even you are confused. Your only option is to face the facts squarely, admit your errors, and make them right.

2: You have managed to burn your bridges with everyone who might help you. Even worse, you cannot make it on your own. It's a good time, therefore, to start making amends and cultivating friends.

1: If you study your circumstances, you will find that someone stands ready to help you—if you change your attitude and ask for assistance.

Unchanging: Your pessimistic attitude leaves little room for hope and growth. You kill opportunities before they can even arise. You need to reassess these deadly, arrogant attitudes.

55. Maturity

The goal of human living is not just to live a full life, be a nice person, and die. Just as a god in ancient mythology might aspire to control and direct a natural force such as lightning, we are meant to aspire to control and direct a wide range of higher forces: love, wisdom, beauty, peace, joy, power, and so on. But each of these forces contains enormous power—a power which is constructive and benevolent in mature hands, but could be destructive and harmful in evil ones. Whatever lessons we are learning, therefore, the proper goal is always maturity—the ability to express these forces with wisdom, authority, and benevolence. In this circumstance, we need to examine candidly where we are acting in immature, selfish ways—and what it means to act as a true agent of God—a true expression of maturity.

Your Resistance: To whatever degree you can be seduced by the lure of materialistic ideas and values, you will fall short of achieving maturity. This does not mean that you must reject materialism; it means you need to embrace the life of spirit more completely.

Your Next Step: Each time you incorporate more of the life of spirit into your daily thoughts, behavior, and values, you become more mature. You should therefore strive to discover, learn, and master some new aspect of spirit each day of your life.

THE CHANGING LINES

6: Invoke the memory of those who have demonstrated maturity in the past.

5: You are surrounded by immaturity in others. Do not add to it yourself, lest you be drawn into circumstances that quickly deteriorate.

4: You mistake personal charm and brilliance for maturity. You have not achieved as much as you think you have.

3: Do not let your own maturity be tarnished by arrogance or a superior attitude toward others. See the potential for maturity in everyone.

2: This situation calls for mature control of your emotions. Act with generosity, goodwill, and patience, rather than selfishness, anger, and irritation.

1: If you lack maturity in the area of your inquiry, seek out and find someone who possesses it. The ability to recognize genuine spiritual maturity in others is a great attribute.

Unchanging: In your effort to create the appearance of maturity, you have instead created a humorless, grim monster. Try being human again.

56. Experimentation

Much of our growth comes through experimentation. We are given a set of variables to deal with, and have the opportunity to put them together in whatever way makes the most sense to us. Once we see the result, we then evaluate it, learning from our mistakes and building on our inspirations. We often operate under the impression that we have been given *carte blanche.* In reality, however, we will progress most quickly if we can recognize that we are being guided by an ideal plan—and get in the habit of invoking it to help us. In this way, we can link our experiments in living and growing with the inner force of reality. We can take the guesswork out of experimentation and greatly increase our chances for success.

Your Resistance: These experiments in living call on us to bring something new of the inner life into expression into our outer life. You have a tendency to think that the physical plane is all that there is—and ignore spirit. This kind of nearsight-edness leads to many failed experiments.

Your Next Step: Many fine records have been left us of earlier experiments in human living: the various scriptures of the world, inspired writings, and so on. Before going off half-cocked, consult some of the great sages of humanity. See what they recommend in your position, then adapt this advice to suit your needs. If you must experiment, do so wisely!

THE CHANGING LINES

6: Shun the temptation to impose values and ethics on others. Give them the opportunity to learn through experimentation of their own.

5: The sense of alienation that you feel stems from your own rejection of the guidance of the higher self.

4: Be less judgmental of others and more open to creative possibilities.

3: You should reap the benefit of this time of experimentation through a stronger sense of ethics and values.

2: Do not be intimidated by popular opinion. Take the time to develop your own perspectives on issues, and have the courage to voice them.

1: You are operating on snap judgments based on false assumptions. Gather all of the relevant facts before you choose a course of action.

Unchanging: You have become comfortable with a set of expectations and ethics that served you well 20 years ago, but are now out of date. It is time to bring yourself up to date.

57. Sensitivity

Your growth is being guided by the invisible hand of the higher self. To accelerate it, you must therefore become more receptive to the direction and love of the higher self, as it seeks to guide you. This requires the development of your spiritual intuition, preferably through the practice of active medtiation. But sitting in meditation is not enough. It must be blended with the active work of striving to become more sensitive to the higher dimensions within other people, animals, and all life forms. We need to learn that all of life is intelligent, and our principal treasure or resource as a human is consciousness. As we increase our sensitivity to the governing intelligences of life, we gradually become more receptive to the guidance of our own higher self.

Your Resistance: Our lives are structured primarily by our experiences in the physical world. It can be difficult to transcend the limited perspective of the physical plane and register the intuitive guidance of the higher self.

Your Next Step: Learn to rely on the inner knowingness of the spiritual intuition as more reliable and accurate than what your physical senses tell you.

THE CHANGING LINES

6: You are trying to be all things to all people, an impossible task. Try being yourself instead—the best self you can possibly be.

5: Avoid criticizing others or yourself for slowness in learning certain lessons.

4: Whenever you are stumped in your creative work, take the time to invoke the ideal plan.

3: Accept the people you interact with as they are, building from there. Consult their own higher self as you help them grow.

2: You have repressed certain memories and feelings because they were painful. Learn to accept such pain without suffering. Then you can confront the issues that are now too painful to examine.

1: You are too easily offended. Stop taking everything so personally.

Unchanging: Your willful ignorance of the higher self in your daily life borders on superstition. Do not let your mind shrink to such small dimensions.

58. Cheerfulness

Joy is one of the great hallmarks of the spiritual life. It is therefore quite helpful to cultivate a foundation of cheerfulness and good humor as we pursue the various lessons of personal and spiritual growth. For as we grow, we will need to learn to handle conflict and stress, deal with intense energies, and face unpleasant conditions. The ability to approach such lessons cheerfully makes it much easier to work with detachment. A depressed person is unable to grow, at least until he or she conquers the depression. A pessimist is unlikely to see the value of growing—or not define it correctly. A grim person may believe it is his or her duty to grow but the burden of this heavy attitude in effect cancels out any efforts to transcend. The higher self reaches out to us on the wavelength of joy. By cultivating a steadfast attitude of good cheer, even in the face of embarrassment or discouragement, we keep the gates open for the guidance and help of the higher self.

Your Resistance: Spiritual authorities have brainwashed us for centuries into believing that dourness is the true posture of the spiritual aspirant. You must shed such prudery before you will be able to cultivate a full measure of cheerfulness.

Your Next Step: As cheerfulness blossoms in your character, strive to become aware of how the joy of the higher self is nurturing and sustaining it.

146

THE CHANGING LINES

6: Creative achievement brings you a sense of joy that draws you closer than ever to the higher self.

5: Share your cheerfulness with others by encouraging them to seize their opportunities for growth.

4: You are letting your efforts to serve be tarnished by grimness and excessive severity. This can create more harm than good.

3: The call for cheerfulness is not the same as hedonism. Take care not to overindulge in materialistic pleasures.

2: You are brooding too much over things you cannot change. Lighten up! Celebrate the blessings you enjoy.

1: Take time to enjoy God's handiwork in nature and your own life. This helps connect you to the inner resources of joy.

Unchanging: You have a tendency to be blinded by bliss at times, to the point where it distorts your perceptions of the motives and acts of other people. Do not be conned by your own innate cheerfulness and optimism.

59. Universalism

The lessons confronting you are not especially personal lessons; they are lessons that the whole of humanity is struggling to learn as well. In order to understand fully the lesson you should be learning, and how to apply it, you need to see it within the larger context of humanity as a whole. Your personal efforts to enlighten the mind, for example, will be conditioned and restricted by the willingness of society to let individuals think for themselves. Your efforts to express goodwill toward others may be severely limited if you grew up in an ethnic background that preaches hostility and suspicion. At present, your efforts to grow are being impeded by exactly this kind of cultural blind spot—or the immaturity of mass consciousness itself. To overcome it, you must realize that the true universal connection with humanity exists at the level of the higher self, not through racial, cultural, or national ties.

Your Resistance: Your strong loyalty to your racial, ethnic, or cultural heritage has restricted your ability to cultivate an objective, universal perspective.

Your Next Step: You must break out of your "We're right, they're wrong" mode of thinking about current events and other people. Instead, teach yourself to think in terms of "What is best for everyone involved?"

THE CHANGING LINES

6: Your efforts have placed you in some jeopardy. Nothing more can be done at the moment. The best course of action is to withdraw.

5: Encourage friends and associates to transcend their separativeness and find a common ground of agreement.

4: You have the opportunity to heal schisms and promote goodwill among various groups. Seize it!

3: It is easy to spot faults and criticize others for their ideas and efforts—but it is not much of a contribution. You need to become a positive force.

2: Learn to treat the people who oppose you with goodwill and respect. They have a legitimate point of view, too.

1: Your idea of commitment or service is to jump on a popular bandwagon. You need to understand that "causes" divide people, not unite them. Try to become a healing force instead.

Unchanging: As long as you view yourself as the child of a certain national, ethnic, religious, or racial group, you will be unable to grow significantly. You must come to realize that you are a child of God—as is everyone else, regardless of their religious or cultural practices. Stop creating unnecessary divisions.

60. Unwritten Rules

You are coming head to head with unspoken censorship. In your efforts to transcend the limits of society and cultural thinking, you are discovering that mass consciousness enforces certain unwritten rules that you are expected to know and observe, even though they are never discussed. It is probably not a good idea to battle these taboos or limitations directly. Instead, redefine what you are trying to do. Instead of challenging the cherished rules of social action, devote yourself to embracing the principles of divine action. Restrain yourself to reconciling your own thoughts and attitudes to cosmic ideals. As you learn to express these divine laws more and more powerfully in your individual life, they will become a quiet but noble example for others—and society—to follow.

Your Resistance: Once we glimpse the ideal, we want to reform society as quickly as possible. Often, we forget to reform ourself first. As a result, we take on a lot of unnecessary (but justified) opposition.

Your Next Step: Even though you understand the universal implications of your lesson, direct your primary attention toward making things right in your own mental household and personal conduct. For the moment, leave the ills of society to be the plaything of those who do not understand as much.

THE CHANGING LINES

6: You may have to challenge some manmade rules in order to serve the plan of God. Do so quietly, without drawing attention to yourself.

5: Others turn to you for guidance. They sense the authority of your insights. If you do not betray their trust, there is much good that you can do.

4: You are being too enthusiastic in demanding that others toe the line. Try developing some compassion.

3: It is admirable to develop a strong set of values to guide your life. It is not admirable to try to impose them on others. Do not become a rulemaker yourself. Encourage others to think for themselves.

2: You are way too arrogant in your moral certainty. If you have a truly universal perspective, you will respect the myriad of ways groups and nations try to express the divine insight they have had.

1: Just as you cannot fight city hall, it is a poor idea to try to confront mass consciousness directly. Be content with reforming yourself.

Unchanging: You are dealing in an area where social opinion is largely unformed. Part of your responsibility is to make sure that the ideas and attitudes that emerge in human awareness will be based on spiritual truths, not superstitions.

61. Virtue

In the Old Testament, the word "virtue" has a special meaning. It refers to the state of perfect attunement between the mind and the character on the one hand and the spiritual self on the other hand. A virtuous person is not just one who follows all of the rules and dogma of his or her faith, therefore, but also one who has direct and ongoing contact with spirit. Few people have achieved perfect virtue, but everyone who professes interest in spiritual growth should be striving for it. Indeed, the lessons you are dealing with are important ones for the development of virtue. They challenge you to act with as much of the wisdom and benevolence of the higher self that you can, in spite of what may be happening in outer events. Whatever the nature of the problem, the solution lies in attuning to and trusting in the wisdom of the higher self to guide us to a mature, virtuous resolution.

Your Resistance: As the personality develops skills and talents in the art of living, it becomes tempting to rely on this mundane knowledge to solve the problems before it. There is often a great reluctance to be guided by the wisdom of the higher self.

Your Next Step: It is not enough just to know about spirit and its qualities; we must integrate them into our values and guiding principles, so that we become a person of virtue.

THE CHANGING LINES

6: Do not overestimate your spiritual strength, even though it is growing. Keep in mind that you are still a human being.

5: Your inner strength sustains not only your growth but also the growth of many who follow you.

4: The force of virtue within you will bring you into touch with people of similar development. They can help you.

3: You are confusing emotional moods for virtue and principle. Just because you like something does not make it right. You need to search a bit more deeply in your inner life to find the source of virtue.

2: You have hammered shut your conscience and will not listen to it. Until you unfasten the nails and let it guide you again, all future growth is halted.

1: Be guided by the spiritual principles and truths of your religious or cultural heritage.

Unchanging: The wisdom you can tap so readily is meant to be shared with others, to stimulate them to think more clearly. Do not begrudge them the help they seek.

62. Good Works

It is not enough just to be a person of high virtue, as described in Hexagram 61; that is but half of the role we must play. As we grow spiritually, we must follow through on the virtue we acquire, and translate it into good works. We must ground heaven on earth. This is the lesson before you now. Having contacted and been inspired by goodwill, harmony, peace, or joy, how do you translate these abstract divine forces into service that enriches life on earth? It is not enough just to pray for peace; you must actively involve yourself in becoming a peacemaker. It is not enough just to preach nonviolence; you must actively participate in healing the wounds of bigotry and hate that separate groups of people here on earth. The challenge to you is to find ways to activate and express the plan of heaven to meet the needs of humanity and the planet.

Your Resistance: Many spiritual aspirants ignore the challenge of good works by protesting that they are not advanced enough to understand the divine plan. It is not necessary to understand the whole plan before taking action to play your part. If nothing else, you can always try fulfilling the golden rule.

Your Next Step: It is our duty to become an agent of spirit on earth. We should be constantly trying to expand our role of helpfulness and sacrifice. This is the surest way to open new opportunities for growth.

THE CHANGING LINES

6: Do not be surprised if your unselfish service to others leads to a measure of recognition.

5: It is not the work you are doing that counts, but rather the attitude with which you do it. Be sure to enrich life through your good works, not curse it with a chip on your shoulder.

4: Your "holier than thou" attitude is estranging you from your best opportunities for good works.

3: If sacrifice is called for, do not hesitate to make it. Your sacrifice will lead to new opportunities.

2: Once you take on a duty or obligation, fulfill it as best you can.

1: Do not resent the restrictions of circumstance; they define the ideal scope of your good works and service.

Unchanging: Beware the temptation to let personal motives and selfish ambition obscure the true value of your good works.

63. The Ideal

The I Ching concludes with two hexagrams that sum up the entire drama of duality: The Ideal (#63) and The Actual (#64). The ideal represents the perfect alignment of all forces in a situation—heaven brought to earth. The actual represents the way conditions on earth are at present. But this does not make the actual the opposite of the ideal—just its working partner. After all, the current, actual conditions contain the seed of the ideal, plus the divine momentum to reach it. When Hexagram 63 comes up in regard to personal growth, it indicates that you need to become more familiar with the divine ideals of life at their own level—i.e., the level of spirit. Instead of talking about love, you need to contact and express love. You need to learn to use it as a healing, building force. Instead of longing for beauty, you need to become an agent of divine beauty, starting with your own self-expression. You cannot expect to make the actual conditions of your life completely ideal—but you are meant to contact and integrate as much as possible of the ideal into your daily efforts to grow.

Your Resistance: There is a tendency to emphasize the gap between the actual and the ideal and become depressed. This is counterproductive.

Your Next Step: The ideal is not a utopian, "garden of Eden" state of life. Ideals are living, moving divine forces which exist now. They await your use.

THE CHANGING LINES

6: Stop carrying the burdens and woes of the world on your shoulders. They cannot bear the load. Learn to share this responsibility with the whole of life.

5: The sense of emptiness that you feel is the result of not having cultivated an awareness of the rich, spiritual life within.

4: Your behavior has been less than ideal. You need to clean up your own act before pointing the finger elsewhere.

3: Your cynicism is a brittle shell which will break when you try to lean on it for support. Look for support from higher levels.

2: Your dreams of perfection are actually counter-productive. They are setting you up for bitter disappointment.

1: You are being a bit naïve in your approach to this situation. The promises of growth and progress cannot be realized so quickly.

Unchanging: Others look up to you. Do not betray their trust in you.

64. The Actual

It is often depressing, or at least discouraging, to contemplate the state of world affairs. Ongoing warfare in almost every continent. Starvation. Greed. Religious groups that fight one another. It is enough to make a person a pessimist. And this is just the problem. Too many people have looked at life with a jaundiced eye and chosen to believe that it is a pretty awful place. This is what is known as the illusion of the actual. To some degree, you have succumbed to it. You have forgotten that within the actual conditions of life lies the seed of the ideal—and the power to implement it. There are serious problems that humanity must face. But it is no service to mankind to magnify these problems and distort their relevance. It is time to stop being the critic and start assuming some responsibility for cleaning up the mess. And the ideal place to begin is by eliminating the pessimism, despondency, and hopelessness that has characterized your thinking and behavior before.

Your Resistance: You have let your mind be held hostage by the group minds of various limited thinkers. You will have to detach from your mental slavery before anything else can be done.

Your Next Step: Strive for balance in assessing life on earth and its achievements. If you give the progress of humanity equal time with its problems, you will find the curse of pessimism losing its grip.

THE CHANGING LINES

6: Be sure to take time to celebrate the wisdom and insight you are gaining by handling this situation with maturity and sensibility.

5: Do not be discouraged by slow progress. You may be surprised by what happens if you stick with plans.

4: Do not let hostility color a disagreement you are having with others. You will need their help later on.

3: Your sense of discouragement is more the product of immaturity and inexperience than impossibility. Consider other approaches.

2: You are having an intense emotional reaction to conditions which are actually benevolent, not threatening. Calm down and reassess everything.

1: Once you clear away the debris of cynicism and hopelessness, the solution you seek will be much easier to recognize.

Unchanging: There is far greater opportunity in the current conditions of your life than you understand. You are going to be stuck with these conditions until you learn the lessons involved.

I CHING ON LINE

This book, *Changng Lines,* is the complete text of the growth module for *I Ching On Line,* a computer program adapting the I Ching to personal computers. *I Ching On Line* is available in versions both for the Macintosh and IBM PC (and compatibles).

The complete package includes the program plus four modules. The four modules are: the healing module, the decision making module, the relationships module, and the personal growth module. The program plus all four modules can be ordered as a package for $100.

To order the complete *I Ching On Line,* send a check or money order to Ariel Press, 14230 Phillips Circle, Alpharetta, GA 30201 or call toll free, 1-800-336-7769, Monday through Thursday, 8 a.m. to 6 p.m., and charge the order to VISA, MasterCard, or American Express. In Georgia, please add 6 percent sales tax.

Changing Lines, Connecting Lines, Ruling Lines, and *Healing Lines* can also be bought and used independently of the computer program. These books may be bought for $7.95 apiece (plus $1.50 for shipping), or $30 for the set of four, postpaid.

In ordering the computer program, please specify the size of floppy disk and system being used.